Murder, Mystery & Mayhem
in the North East

by Lorna Windham

Also by Lorna Windham

Crime and Punishment
in the North East
(published in 2010)

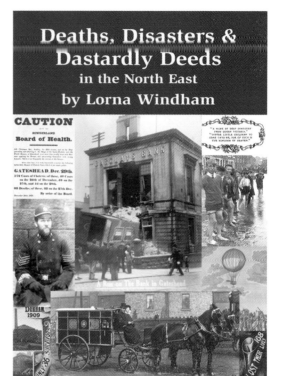

Deaths, Disasters & Dastardly Deeds
in the North East
(published 2012)

Summerhill Books

Summerhill Books publishes local history books on
Northumberland, Durham and Tyneside.

To receive a catalogue of our titles, send a stamped addressed envelope to:

Andrew Clark, Summerhill Books,
PO Box 1210, Newcastle upon Tyne NE99 4AH

or email: summerhillbooks@yahoo.co.uk

or visit our website:

www.summerhillbooks.co.uk

Copyright Lorna Windham 2014

First published in 2014 by

Summerhill Books
Newcastle upon Tyne

ISBN: 978-1-906721-88-6

Contents

Acknowledgements

I would like to thank two brilliant super sleuths and genealogists: John Gallon and Jill Forster for their detective work; Diane Gray, Community Development Officer from Hive Radio and Bede's World for her photographs and setting me on the trail of transported Jarrow miners; Margaret McDonald from Hebburn and Jarrow History Society for sharing David Ridley's Doctoral thesis and shedding light on the 1831 miners' strike; Julie Hogg and Debbie Nyhuis, descendants of Bartholomew Stephenson, for sharing their research; Yvonne Young, Ian and Wendy McArdle and Wendy and Pete Breckon for their support; Matthew Bryson for allowing me to transcribe his 18th century handbill; Ewen and Natasha Windham for their photographs; David for being David; my publisher Andrew Clark for his unswerving guidance and support and, of course, my family.

Picture Credits
Summerhill Books would like to thank the following who kindly gave us images to use in this publication: Alan Brett, John Carlson, Tom Hutchinson, George Nairn, Jim Pace, Ernest Storey, Durham Miners' Association, Gateshead Library, West Newcastle Picture History Collection and Beamish – North of England Open Air Museum,

Mayhem in Silksworth, County Durham, 1891. Striking miners felt that deputies were more favourably treated if they did not join the union. The owners believed that union members pressured the deputies until they joined. Lord Londonderry, owner of the colliery and the pitmen's houses, evicted the miners and their families by employing Hartlepool, 'candy men' he stationed at Candy Hall Farm. They were escorted by police into Silksworth every morning, supposedly to 'shift timber' to the accompaniment of singing villagers, the banging of pots and pans and people from Sunderland throwing stones. Miners from other collieries struck in support of Silksworth and almost brought the Durham coalfield to a standstill. After a four month stalemate work began again in March 1891.

Introduction

Most of us know little of the murky criminal underworld and its murderers. Many of us enjoy mysteries, but do not believe in the supernatural and the majority of us have never experienced the horror of invasion and war.

Murder is deliberate and premeditated. It is the most serious offence under common law in England and Wales. The intent to murder was originally called malice aforethought, though the act required neither malice nor premeditation. The subject of murder holds a fascination for many people who are curious, frightened, thrilled or horrified at the thought of the foul deeds perpetrated by their fellows. Some may even enjoy the salacious gossip which surfaces round a crime involving blood and gore.

Through the centuries our ancestors attended hangings, read confessions, listened to dark ballads, read penny dreadfuls and bought souvenirs. Our generation watch murder dramas, and play games like 'Cluedo or 'Murder'. We cannot seem to get enough of the horror of this dreadful crime.

Centuries ago Sir Edward Coke defined the act of murder. He held public offices under Elizabeth I, James I and Charles I. As Chief Justice he wrote 'The Institutes of the Lawes of England' which have been described as 'almost the foundation of the law'. His frequently cited definition of the actus reus ('wrongful act') of murder is below:

'Murder is when a man of sound memory and of the age of discretion, unlawfully killeth within any county of the realm any reasonable creature in rerum natura (a life in being) under the king's peace, with malice aforethought, either expressed by the party or implied by the law. So as the party wounded, or hurt etc. within a day of the same.'

A mystery, on the other hand, baffles us because it cannot be easily explained and most of us like a conundrum. The unexplained, the unanswerable captures the imagination and makes us return to it again and again. Treasure hoards, rock carvings, supernatural events, strange happenings, to name a few arouse our curiosity because there is an enigmatic quality about them.

However, there is nothing enigmatic about fear aroused when an ordered and stable world disintegrates in terror. The North East, as a border region, has had more than its fair share of turmoil though the centuries. Wars, invasions, mutinies, industrial accidents: that's mayhem!

These tales of murder, mystery and mayhem are set in the North East. Some describe deadly acts, others will haunt you and one or two are rip-roaring adventures which put Hollywood and the world of film to shame.

www.lornawindham.co.uk

Right: A medieval drying out coffin (used to allow bodies to decay before they were buried in church) in St Paul's Church, Jarrow.

Section One – Murders

'.. why is it that scarcely any are executed but the poor?' Thomas Paine

18th Century Murders

Punishment was savage between the late 17th and early 19th centuries under the English Legal System called the Bloody Code. Murder was a hanging offence. Perhaps that is why Thomas Topham took his own life.

Gateshead in the 19th century.

Topham Strongman Murder
April 21st, 1739

The ironically named Thomas Topham was a strongman from Clapham who performed in Gateshead. His act is outlined below in a notice to the public:

'For the benefit of Thomas Topham, the strong man, from Islington, whose performances have been looked upon by the Royal Society and several persons of distinction, to be the most surprising, as well as curious, of anything performed in England; on which account, as other entertainments are more frequently met with than what he proposes, he humbly hopes gentlemen and ladies, &c., will honour him with their presence at the Nags-head, in Gateshead, on Monday, the 23rd of this instant, at four o'clock, where he intends to perform several feats of strength, viz:- He bends an iron poker, three inches in circumference, over his arm; and one of two inches and a quarter, round his neck; he breaks a rope that will bear two thousand weight, and with his fingers rolls up a pewter dish of seven pounds hard metal; he lays the back part of his head on one chair, and his heels on another, and suffering four men to stand on his body, he moves them up and down at pleasure; he lifts a table six feet in length by his teeth, with a half hundred weight hanging at the further end of it; and lastly, to oblige the publick, he will lift a butt full of water. Each person to pay one shilling.'

Apparently ten years later on August 10th, 1749, Topham became jealous. When *'master of a publick house in Shoreditch, London, he stabbed his wife, then cut his own throat and stabbed himself, after which he lived two days.'* (Sykes, Vol. I, p. 156.)

Topham was obviously enraged beyond all reasoning. Was this what happened to William Smith?

Boy Watches Father Hanged!
September 13th, 1739

Fifty-three year old, William Smith from Berwick-on-Tweed murdered his wife. Though he *'made some small confession'* to Reverend Mr Wilkinson, on the Town Moor gallows in Newcastle, Smith, with rope round his neck, stated that if anything were *'printed as his dying speech, it would be false ...'* He was described as being hardened and unconcerned about facing death, though he requested his clothes be given to his thirteen year old son *'who stood by him at his execution.'* (Sykes, Vol I, p.157.)

The child in the following story was given no chance of life.

Child Murderer
August 8th, 1757

'William Heugh was executed in Durham, pursuant to his sentence, for the murder of a bastard child.' (Sykes, Vol I, p. 218.)

Old cobbled steps in Moatside Lane, Durham.

A lane or vennel off Saddler Street, Durham.

Occasionally one man is murdered by another and history does not record the reason.

Byers' Death
August 9th, 1762

Thomas Coulson murdered Thomas Byers. Coulson was executed for the deed at Durham. Coulson and Byers appear to have been working class men.

However, Mr James, in the following account worked in the legal profession.

Murder at Alnwick Fair
July 29th, 1771

It is usual to find an attorney on the right side of the law. Mr James was an attorney from Morpeth. According to one account, James was partial to a drink and was cutting gingerbread with a knife. A Constable Bolam told him off because of his loud behaviour and James stabbed Bolam in the chest. Bolam stood for a few minutes, collapsed and died an hour later. The coroner's verdict was wilful murder and James was held in Morpeth Gaol.

A second account states that James had taken a knife out of his pocket and was cutting and giving away the gingerbread for free. The stallholder, not knowing him, called a constable and James knifed him. Whatever the truth of the matter, James was

brought before the assizes in 1772 and found guilty of manslaughter.

Left:
A picturesque view of Alnwick in the 19th century.

Alcohol is often the key factor in manslaughter, but Robert Storey was sober and found an unsuspecting victim.

'Cockle Geordie'
August 18th, 1783

Thomas Idle was given the nickname 'Cockle Geordie' because he sold cockles. He must have had many customers on one particular day as he had several guineas which were seen by others in a public house. Robert Storey waited his opportunity to rob and murder Idle. Storey succeeded in his purpose, but was caught, convicted and executed at Durham.

Right: This sign is above the Market Tavern (once the City Tavern), Durham.

Man has always been inventive and no more so when murder is intended.

MARKET TAVERN

THIS PUB WAS ORIGINALLY CALLED THE CITY TAVERN.

A SERIES OF EVENTS SINCE 1850 ENSUED THE POPULARITY OF THIS PUB. THIS IS THE STORY.

IN 1851 AN ACT OF PARLIAMENT ALLOWED MEAT, FISH AND POULTRY TO BE TRADED IN THE MARKET PLACE SO THAT THE AREA BECAME THE FOCAL POINT OF THE CITY.

IN 1853 THE COUNCIL COMMITTEE OF DURHAM DECLARED THE WATER IN THE MARKET PLACE UNFIT FOR HUMAN CONSUMPTION SO THAT CUSTOMERS COULD ONLY QUENCH THEIR THIRST FROM THE EXCELLENT ALES SERVED IN THIS PUBLIC HOUSE.

IN 1865 THE CITY TAVERN WAS RE-NAMED THE MARKET HOTEL AND IT GREW EVEN MORE POPULAR IN 1871 WHEN THE DURHAM MINERS ASSOCIATION WAS FORMED HERE

THE MARKET HOTEL BECAME SO SUCCESSFUL THAT BY 1940 IT WAS THE ONLY REMAINING PUB IN THE MARKET PLACE.

TODAY THE MARKET TAVERN IS MAINTAINING IT'S TRADITION AS A VERY POPULAR PLACE TO SAMPLE THE FINEST SELECTION OF THE NATION'S ALES.

WELCOME

Woman Hanged For Murder
July 22nd, 1799

Mary Nicholson poisoned her mistress who died. On being convicted of murder, Mary was sentenced to be hanged at Durham. She stood on a cart, but the rope broke. When she fell to the ground she was still alive. Some might assume that justice and sentence had been carried out at this point, apparently not. Two hours later a stouter rope was found and she was hanged for a second time. This time the rope held.

The law appeared inflexible when dealing with adults, but could be more merciful where children were concerned. Children have always played and sometimes disagreed. This led to unfortunate consequences in 1831.

19th Century Murders
Boys at Play
June 1st, 1831

A number of boys were playing in Gallowgate, Newcastle. George Hills threw the sole of a clog at Robert Carnaby Dobson and killed him. George pleaded guilty. He was sentenced, because of his good character, to be imprisoned for one calendar month.

Life was hard, so it must have been nice to relax and go to a local fair, buy a memento and have a drink with friends.

Death by Sword Stick
November 8th 1838

Joseph Purdie, a farm servant had been to Morpeth fair with his friends and bought a sword stick (with a concealed blade). On the way home they stopped at the Astley Arms near Cramlington. Ralph Stanley, a pitman from Holywell Colliery joined them in a drink of ale.

When they left the public house there was a quarrel between Purdie and Stanley over the sword stick. Purdie stabbed Stanley giving him a six inch wound in his abdomen. Before he fell to the ground, Stanley punched Purdie twice. Stanley died, but Purdie was acquitted of manslaughter at the Assizes.

Market day in Morpeth in the 19th century.

The disposal of a body has always presented problems. Burning, unless at an extremely high temperature, leaves bones. Burial meant it could be dug up by animals and putting it in a river also had its difficulties.

A Hammer Blow
July 13th 1839

When a body wearing only a flannel shirt and stockings and tied with rope weighted by a stone was found floating in the River Wear, it was taken to Monkwearmouth's workhouse. Johann Friedrich Berckholtz was the 55 year old captain of the 'Phoenix' from Stettin, moored on the Wear. Two of Berckholtz's crew identified the body as being his.

The quayside at Sunderland in the 1880s.

The captain's cabin was searched and bore evidence of the deed. Suspicion fell on the mate, Friedrich Ehlert and the 19 year old cabin boy, Daniel Muller. They both admitted they had been accomplices, but each blamed the other for the deed. Muller was a witness for the Crown at Durham Assizes. He said that on the evening of the 11th, Ehlert had given him spirits. Whilst Muller had held the lantern, Ehlert hit the captain three times over the head with a hammer. They had both then lowered the body by rope into the river, got in a boat and rowed to a bridge dragging the body behind them. The mate had tied a stone to the body and let it sink. The rest of the crew corroborated Muller's story. Ehlert protesting his innocence to the last was convicted and executed at Durham on August 16th.

Berckholtz was a ship's captain and we will never know why he was murdered.

However, when two men had different work ethics and one is in charge of the other there was bound to be conflict.

A Sledge Hammer
February 22nd, 1842

'Messrs Edward Lumsden and Son', manufacturers of chains and anchors, in Strand Street, Monkwearmouth, regarded their foreman, James Liddle, as one of the best workmen in the area. He had worked for them for 28 years.

Liddle was doing his job, telling off workman James Robertson for not working. Robertson then hit Liddle on the head with a 6lb sledge hammer. Liddle was carried home with a fractured skull and brain damage. He died at 5 o'clock the following morning. Robertson was arrested, placed before Lord Denton at the Durham Summer Assizes and sentenced to transportation for life.

The following two stories are of murders, committed within months of each other. They have similarities as they involve drunken young men in their early twenties who were involved in scuffles which led to two deaths. They suffered the full sentence of the law at the same time, date and place and had to endure a bungled public hanging.

The first story is set around the building of the Newcastle and Berwick Railway in 1846, which was to be an important northern artery connecting the city and the important border town of Berwick. Work would have attracted men seeking employment from all over Great Britain.

The Wrecked Wagon
October 5th, 1846

Daniel, better known as Dan, Hives, was apparently from Oxfordshire and tipsy when he drove a wagon into a ditch on October 5th. He had been employed as a waggoner at Long Benton on the Newcastle and Berwick Railway line almost since work on it began. John Todd, agent to Messrs Rush and Lawton, railway contractors described Hives as, ' ... *a stout little fellow and very much respected,*' and ' ... *a quiet man.*'

Miners' cottages at Long Benton.

Todd went on to say that English and Irish labourers were employed on the railway and there had been a number of disagreements between the two groups. There were disturbances according to William Oliver as the Irish labourers worked for lower wages than the English. Unfortunately, there were a lot of unemployed Englishmen.

Irishmen George Matthews aged 20, a navigator, and John Hughes aged 25 worked on the same railway line as Hives. Hughes had lodged with widow, Mary Curry at Camperdown just over two miles from Long Benton and had been there about a month. She said he went to work on Monday, October 5th at 7 am and Hughes returned with Matthews before 12. They had dinner, said they were going to Hartlepool and Hughes told her to get his clothes ready. The men left just after noon.

Matthews had lodged for a month in the autumn with Mary Storey as well as her mother and sister at Killingworth Colliery just over a mile from Long Benton. Mary said Matthews left to go to work on Monday, October 5th at 6.30 am and returned with a stranger at 2 pm. He gathered his clothes together in a handkerchief and said he was, *'going upon a tramp'.*

That afternoon Hives brought two wagons from Walker Quay to the stables near Long Benton, whilst William Oliver, a wagon driver, was driving on the Bank Head. Oliver had known Hives for about 18 months and was told to assist him because he was '*tipsy'*. When they were near the top of Benton Lane the second wagon became stuck in a ditch. Oliver tried to help Hives, but the wagon would not budge.

Oliver ran ahead along the Coach Road about 100 yards round a bend to the first wagon so he could use one of the two horses to rescue Hive's wagon. At approximately 2-3 pm Oliver passed Matthews and Hughes coming from Long Benton and noted the taller man carried a bundle. Stopping the wagon, Oliver uncoupled one of the horses and started to walk back to Hives and the second wagon. It took five minutes for Oliver to return. Hives was no longer wearing his cap, jacket or waistcoat and his face was covered in blood. Matthews and Hughes were within ten yards, but walking away from Hives and Oliver.

Hives said something to Oliver which he did not hear. But it would appear Matthews and Hughes had assaulted Hives. Oliver leapt on a horse and the men started to run. Hives told Oliver to ride after them, until he could get help. Hives followed Oliver at a run. Oliver came abreast of Matthews and Hughes after about a

Two stone built houses in Long Benton.

11

quarter of a mile. One jumped to the side and hit Oliver with a stick. There would be a mark on his back for at least a fortnight afterwards. Oliver carried on until he reached the railway bridge and got three men to return with him, but could not see Hives, Matthews or Hughes.

Dorothy Bell, wife of James Bell, lived in Benton Cottage, Long Benton Lane. There were two cottages between her and a Captain Potts' home. Dorothy was disturbed by the uproar and hearing swearing watched from her garden wicket. She saw two running men, one with a bundle, another following them in his shirt and a third man galloping behind on horseback. Tracking them by running down a field almost to the wagon way, she heard nothing she could distinguish, but watched them all go down the wagon way and along the lane.

Joseph Scott, a waggoner at Coxlodge Colliery, and Mary Brason, who lived at Willington Quay, verified Dorothy's testimony. Scott added that he saw Hives with a bloody face and in his shirt from about 500 yards away. He heard Hives shout at the men, but did not hear what he said.

Matthews and Hughes continued on their journey until they reached the end of Captain Potts' Lane. Matthews put his bundle on the ground and ran towards Hives. Hives then ran towards Scott. Matthews retreated towards Hughes and turned into Potts' Lane. Hives followed them, but then stopped to talk to Scott and Mary Brason, before continuing his chase. Mary ran with him until they arrived at Captain Potts' farm.

Mary said that the men had passed her in Potts' Lane and Hives had stopped and talked to her before he ran after the men again. With Hives about five yards behind them, Matthews and Hughes came to a stone stile on the left side of the lane. One of the men said to Hives, 'You b – r, if you follow any further, I will finish you.' The men crossed the stile and Hives and Mary followed suit.

George Matthews, aged 20 and John Hughes, aged 25.

Captain Potts, a Northumberland magistrate, was in one of his fields. He heard Hughes issue verbal threats. It was at this time Potts saw a dishevelled and bloody faced Hives. Potts held Hives back. Hives tried to get past Potts saying, 'Now we have you,' and 'Master you'll assist me – you'll not see an Englishman murdered by two Irishmen.'

Potts told the men to explain what had occurred. Hughes raised his stick and moved forwards repeating his previous threat. Hives and Potts walked slowly towards him, whilst Potts stated that they would not get away as he would follow them himself.

The men continued to walk on followed by Potts who was holding Hives' shirt. When they came near an enclosed footpath, Hives again tried to get close to Matthews and Hughes, but Potts prevented him.

Matthews put his bundle down and made as if to button his braces. He then stood upright, with his bundle under his left arm and his right hand hidden behind his shirt and waistcoat. He walked past Hughes towards Hives and Potts. Potts had raised his right arm to prevent Hughes attacking him and Matthews' shoulder touched Potts' right arm.

Potts heard Matthews say, 'Take that you b – r.' He also saw Matthews draw his clenched right hand from beneath his waistcoat and strike Hives. He had no idea Matthews had used a knife. Hives turned to Potts and said, 'Oh dear!' whilst covering his lower bowels with his hand. Matthews and Hughes ran off together.

Potts tried to persuade Hives to join him in chasing after the men, but Hives said, *'Oh dear, master, look at the blood, how it is going out at my foot.'* Potts, seeing Hives was dying, sat him down and ran after the men. Mary Bryson arrived to see Hives lying in *'a pool of blood'*. He breathed twice and died with Mary by his side.

It was 3.30 pm when Potts watched Matthews and Hughes part at the junction of two footpaths. Hughes walked on the one leading to Heaton Middle Pit and Matthews went on the one to Byker Hill.

Running to the Newcastle and Earsdon Turnpike, Potts told William Blenkinsopp, a butcher, who was out walking, what had happened. After giving him Matthew's description, Blenkinsopp agreed to follow Matthews. Potts also sent people in different directions after Matthews and Hughes.

Hughes appeared to have thrown away a pair of trousers at Heaton Middle Pit. By the time Potts returned to Dog Kennel Field, Hives was dead. When Potts went on to Byker Police Station, Matthews had been arrested. Apparently Blenkinsopp had found Matthews and reported his whereabouts to Ouseburn Police Station.

At 1 am the following day Hughes was apprehended in Sunderland. He had tried to evade arrest by swopping caps with another man and threatened the policeman who arrested him. Hughes was taken to Potts' house where he was identified. Hughes said to Potts, *'You never saw me strike the man; it was the little fellow who shoved the knife into him.'* At 5.50 pm on the way to Benton, Hughes asked the policeman if Hives was dead. Hughes repeated that it was not him, *'but the little man who struck him with the knife.'* He said he had told Matthews it was wrong and that they would be captured.

The double bladed knife that killed Hives was found by John Turner from Newcastle Police Station. It was rusty and open about 150 yards from Hive's body. Thomas Common, the surgeon at Stannington found that Hives had a one inch wound in his abdomen. The femoral artery had been split and the femoral vein holed. He would have died in seconds.

Matthews and Hughes were charged with the wilful murder of Daniel Hives. *'Matthews was arraigned as the principal, and Hughes as an accessory after the fact.'* Hughes was found not guilty and Matthews was convicted of *'Wilful Murder'*. A memorial was forwarded to the government praying a commutation of the sentence. This was not granted. George Matthews received the sentence of death on the February 28th, 1847 for the murder of Daniel Hives on October 7th, 1846. (*Newcastle Courant, March 5th, 1847*).

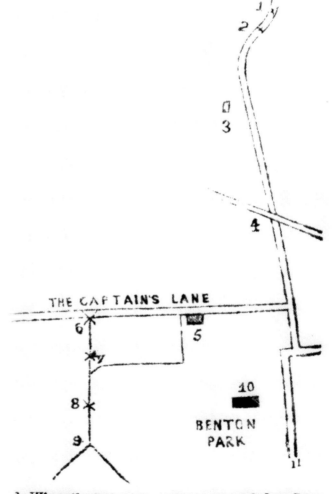

1. Where the first waggon stopped, 610 yards from Long Benton.
2. Where 2nd. waggon got into ditch, 700 yds. from do.
3. Mrs. Bell's cottage, 150 yards from waggon.
4. Coxlodge waggon-way, 325 yds. from Mrs Bell's cottage.
5. Benton farm offices, 455 yards from the waggon-way,
6. Stile, 319 yards from Benton Farm Offices.
7. Place where murder was committed, 98 yards from the stile.
8. Place where knife was found.
9. Where the foot-roads part, and where the men separated.
10. Benton Park, the residence of Captain Potts.
11. Benton Lane.
The whole distance from where the parties first met, to where the murder was committed in the Dog Kennel Field, is about 1,350 yards.

Plan of the locality by C.S. Bell, land surveyor.

13

The second story took place in the Northumberland countryside.

The Christening and the Corpse
February 27th, 1847

Thomas Proud, a labourer, would have expected Sunday, February 7th, 1847, the day of the christening of his youngest child, to be a happy occasion. After all he had invited several neighbours to the church for 2.30 pm. Later they would go to his house at Allerwash for, '... *tea and spirits.*'

The celebration continued when Proud, Robert Brown, William Johnson, Mary Coates, Mary Thompson and Mary Ann Toward went to the Surtees public house at Newbrough and had two peppermint teas. They were the only people in the room, stayed for about three quarters of an hour and left at 7.15 pm.

They were not to know, according to John Pattison, a quarryman who lived at Fourstones railway station, that twenty two year old James Welch was in another room in the same public house drinking with two young men and was, '*tipsy*'.

The christening party started to walk back towards Proud's house when James Welch came out of the Surtees. Benjamin Robson, Robert Robson and Henry Brown appear to have trailed along with Welch.

The Red Lion public house over 150 years ago at Newbrough. It was known as the Surtees by 19th century customers.

A modern photograph of the the Red Lion public house. It dates back to the 1190s and was an old coaching inn.

The witnesses to the Murder

According to Thomas Brown, Welch put his arm round Mary Coates' waist and asked her to go back and drink with him. Brown asked Welch what he wanted. Welch replied he wanted a girl. Brown said it was up to her, but Mary refused Welch's advances. Welch repeated this request to Mary Thompson who also refused. Opposite the Charlton's house, half way between the public house and Mr Ridley's, and without a word, Welch pulled Mary Ann Toward to the ground.

Benjamin Robson, a labourer at Allerwash Redhouse, knew Welch and Proud. He said Welch had hold of Mary Coates at the door of the public house. When Mary Ann Toward was on the ground he hear Proud say to Welch, '*You are interrupting my company and I don't want that tonight.*'

Robson saw Welch and Proud scuffling at Mr Ridley's front gate. When Proud and his group went on, Welch asked Robson to help him off with his coat. The coat was then flung over Robson's arm. Welch followed until Proud got to Mr Ridley's farm gate. There was a struggle between Welch and Proud. Proud was on top of Welch as they traded blows. Proud punched Welch in the back and Welch had his left arm wrapped round Proud, '*striking him with his right hand. Proud pushed Welch down on the road, and kicked him with his foot. He hit him about his left thigh.*'

According to Robert Robson, a servant with Mr Ridley from Newbrough, Welch said, '*Don't kick me when I'm down.*' Henry Brown heard Welch reply, '*Any of you.*' When Proud asked Welch why he was quarrelling with him. Proud then added, '*I don't know you, nor do I want anything to do with you, and you may go about your business.*'

Mary Anne Toward apparently yelled, 'Bob the miller come back, they are murdering Thomas Proud.' Robert Brown returned and asked what the problem was. Proud replied, 'It is a very queer thing that one is to be interrupted by such a vagabond as that.'

Welch stayed on the ground for about 2-3 minutes whilst Proud and his group continued to walk home. Again according to Robert Robson Welch said, 'Wait till I get my neck cloth off.' Welch and several men trailed behind and when they had crossed a footbridge, Welch asked for the loan of a stick. He got one from Robert Robson.

Mary Ann Toward said, 'Welch wasn't running, but he was coming up pretty hard.' When he was three yards away, Welch threw the stick amongst the group. It appeared to hit Proud. According to Mary Ann Toward, Welch used his right hand and struck Proud twice on the left side of his head. Blood flowed immediately. Proud ran about 17 yards and then collapsed with blood flowing from his neck. Mary Ann Toward promptly fainted in the side of a dyke.

Thomas Brown said when Proud fell, Welch ran away, down the hill and over the bridge. Brown went to help Proud, but he was dead.

Benjamin Robson told of a couple of men running past him and he followed walking. He crossed the footbridge again and saw Welch running behind him. Welch shouted, 'Ben I want my coat.' He asked Robson to help him put it on. Robson did this and Welch continued on to the village. From the moment Welch was kicked to the point where he returned for his coat was about 20 minutes.

Henry Brown had returned to the public house when Welch arrived ten minutes later. Brown described Welch as having his waistcoat and neck cloth loose and blood on his breast. Welch asked for a whisky saying he was short of time. He drank it and shook hands with some people, though Brown refused to do so because Welch's hand was covered in blood. Welch started to leave, wished everyone good night, returned, had a word with Hannah Charlton and left.

John Pattison said he was in Head's public house at Fourstones when two young men told him they had been drinking with Welch at the Surtees. A 'tipsy' Welch arrived at 'Head's' about 8 pm. Pattison helped Welch wash off blood. Pattison says Welch swore several times, 'I have let the blood out of the b – r and left him bleeding.' When asked with whom he had been fighting, Welch replied, 'Proud and the miller.' Welch went to the door several times, lay on the settle and slept. Brown watched George Ridley, a farmer and constable from Newbrough, put handcuffs on the sleeping Welch.

Ridley took Welch to Newbrough. He said that Welch had struggled near Head's gardens and nearly pulled him and another man down. Ridley said Welch appeared to be acting as if he was drunk. The next day, Thomas Forster handed Ridley a knife that George Chambers, a labourer from Newbrough, had found in Head's garden. It was identified as the prisoner's.

1. Cottages.
2. Mr. Surtees' public-house, where the parties met.
3. Mr. Ridley's house and farm buildings, near where Welch and Proud had a struggle, as described by the witnesses.
4. Where Welch sat down on the ground.
5. The foot bridge which Welch crossed to get at the deceased, after putting his coat off.
6. The conduit.
7. Where the murder was perpetrated.
8. The place to which the body was removed.
9. The deceased's house.

Plan of the locality.

Robert Charlton, a shoemaker from Newbrough, reported exchanging a coat with Welch a few weeks before the incident, and finding a knife which he returned to him. However, he could not verify whether the knife he was shown was the same as that used in the murder.

The Surgeon's Account

Thomas Coates, a surgeon at Haydon Bridge, examined Proud's body which was lying in a barn. He stated that, *'There was a large incised wound on the left side of the neck, extending from the bottom of the ear to the chin, cut all along. All the soft parts were cut through, extending to the vertebrae; both jugular veins were severed, as was the external carotid artery and the internal carotid artery was almost cut through.'* He felt, *'the knife produced would have inflicted such a wound'* and said, *'it must have been struck with great force.'*

Mr Matthews, addressed the jury on behalf of Welch. He argued, *'... the unfortunate blow was the result of excited passions, under a sense of previous ill-usage in previous conflicts, and particularly from having been kicked when on the ground.'*

The jury was absent for 70 minutes. They found Welch guilty *'... but recommended the prisoner to mercy on the ground of the provocation from the other party.'*

The sentence

Welch received the sentence of death from judge, Mr Baron Alderson for the murder of Thomas Proud, at Warden, near Newbrough, on February 27th, 1847.

Hanging Matthews and Welch

At 8 am, George Matthews and James Welch were led from their cells. Their arms were pinioned and white caps placed on their heads in the porch in front of the governor's house. The under-sheriff and governor of the gaol led the procession consisting of the prisoners each supported by a turnkey and minister. The surgeon, deputy governor and county bailiffs carried white wands to the scaffold in front of the entrance to Morpeth Gaol.

Matthews dressed in a fustian jacket, waistcoat and trousers was clearly ill at ease. His legs trembled, his face was pale and his lips appeared to be repeating the minister's prayer, though what Matthews said was inaudible. He leaned on the turnkey for support.

Welch clothed in a black frock coat, waistcoat and plaid or dark striped trousers moved forward with a firmer step, but his face revealed his suffering.

James Welch, aged 22.

They were both hanged at the same time on March 17th, 1847. According to the 'Hull Packet and East Riding Times' *'... the scene was one of the most sickening and revolting spectacles that ever the eye of man witnessed.'*

The chaplain said a prayer, *'May the God off all goodness have mercy upon you, and according to the multitude of his mercies pardon your every offence against him in thought, word and deed. May he graciously accept your repentance, and may you, for Christ's sake, be with him this day in Paradise. Amen, Amen, Amen.'*

As agreed, on the last, *'Amen'* the trapdoor bolt was released, *'... but through gross mismanagement on the part of the hangman, a superannuated old man named Murdoch belonging to Glasgow, the ropes were just sufficient length to allow the men resting with their feet upon the drop after it has descended, and in that position they remained for a few seconds, when Matthews bent his legs up, and suffered his entire weight to come upon the rope. Welch remained motionless for a brief space and then began stamping and kicking, saying, 'Oh dear, oh dear, Lord have mercy upon me' which he repeated several times. The hangman stood aghast*

16

and everyone appeared struck with horror. At length a cry was raised of, 'hoist them up' and Murdoch seizing the rope that suspended Welch, raised him about a foot and a half, groaning and kicking convulsively. Matthews also was in convulsive action, but not as much as Welch, and he having been raised to the proper height, the hangman seized Welch's legs and holding them close together, threw his whole weight upon them, a position he occupied for several minutes till all struggling was over. Welch lived for 10-15 minutes after the drop fell and Matthews about 6 minutes.'

The newspaper, criticised the end of the prayer as the pre-agreed signal for their, ' ... *ignominious and torturous death ...*' which it described as, ' ... *a scene of such barbarity ... at Morpeth.*' Interestingly the reporter went on to say prophetically, '... *the day must come, and we believe it fast approaching, when a more merciful administration of criminal law will do away forever with the possibility of the recurrence of such a scene of barbarity, when the life which man gave not, by man will not be taken away.*'

('*Freemans Newspaper*', March 20th, 1847. '*Newcastle Courant*', March 5th, 1847. '*Morning Chronicle*', March 1st, 1847. '*Morning Chronicle*', March 3rd, 1847)

Matthews and Welch did not know their victims, but PC Paton did.

PC Paton
May 2nd, 1868

It's strange that John Cruikshanks and David Paton, who had so much in common, should fall out. Both men were Scottish, married with families and members of the Durham police force. They should have been friends as well as colleagues instead their lives were torn apart.

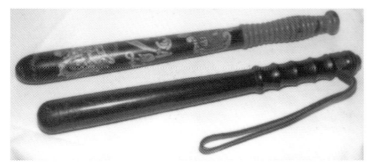 

The basic equipment for police for many years – truncheons and handcuffs.

I suppose Cruikshanks, a member of the Durham County Constabulary at Pittingdon, thought he was doing his duty when he '*lodged information with his superior*' about PC Paton. Paton was already in trouble having earlier been found '*guilty of some irregularities*'. On May 2nd, 1868 Lieutenant-Colonel White ordered Paton to Durham where he received his discharge papers. This should have been the end of the matter, but Paton stayed in Durham probably brooding over what he regarded as the gross injustice perpetrated on him by Cruikshanks.

At 5 pm PC Cruikshanks and McKay finished their shift and started to walk home from Durham. Paton joined them. The walk was peaceful with nothing to indicate the tragedy to follow. On arriving at Sherburn Bridge, Cruikshank decided to take a short cut along the Durham and Sunderland railway line. Paton then said he had information from the Durham office that he needed to hand over to Cruikshanks. This must have sounded plausible as Cruikshanks and McKay accompanied Paton to his village.

McKay, intending to call in for the 'Police Gazette', followed Paton whilst Cruikshanks stayed a wary 20-30 yards from Paton's home. By the time McKay got to Paton's house and sat down, Paton was leaving with his right arm behind his back. Paton's wife shouted, '*He has something!*' McKay looked out of the window to see Paton chasing Cruikshanks in the direction of a public house.

McKay just got outside to see Cruikshanks desperately trying to enter the pub when Paton shot him twice. As he ran to the scene of the murder, McKay watched as Paton put the pistol to his ear and shot himself. Mckay caught him as he fell.

Surgeon, Mr Shaw, was called, but Cruikshanks was dead and Paton died a few minutes later. The Coroner's jury decided that Paton had wilfully murdered Cruikshanks and then committed suicide. There was not enough evidence to make a decision about Paton's sanity. *(T. Fordyce, 1868-75, p. 14-15.)*

Occasionally, sane people do not think of the consequences of their actions.

It Started as a Family Row
January 1st, 1878

When Mary Morton married Thomas Daglish she may have thought she could get on with her in-laws. What occurred at 10.30 am in Shafto Terrace, New Washington did not augur well for Mary's marriage.

Mary was standing at the bottom of the Daglish's yard with her mother Alice. They were using foul language and abusing Mary's mother-in-law who was in her home in Shafto Terrace.

Francis Daglish, Mary's brother-in-law, lived with his parents. He was drunk when Mary's brother, 19 year old George, walked towards them. George was a pitman, sober, and '*shoved*' his mother and sister towards their own home about ten houses from where the Daglish family lived.

However, Mary and her mother returned with half bricks in their hands. Francis came out of his yard and dared them to throw the bricks at him. A brick was thrown, but it missed and Francis struck one of them with his fist.

George came down the row and fought with Francis. On hearing the noise, 57 year old coal miner, James Daglish, Francis' father, came out of his home and saw the men fighting and the women throwing stones at Francis. James tried to stop the brawl and shouted at them all to behave themselves.

The fracas ceased, but Francis went into his house and returned with a poker raised in his hand. While he was away, James had begun to argue with Alice Morton who had fallen to the ground and Mary Daglish was fighting with her mother-in-law. One witness, Thomas Jefferson, a

Front Street, New Washington.

pick sharper, described James as '*laying in*' to Alice Morton. He saw George Morton, ' *... throw more than one half brick; but cannot say whether the first brick hit any one.*' He added that when George saw James Daglish '*... striking Alice Morton on the ground ...*' he threw a brick at James from 5-6 yards away and struck him on the back of the head. James fell on his face and lay still.

Three witnesses, Mrs Walker, the wife of a cartman, Anthony Allsop, a coal hewer, and John Macdonald, a joiner, all from Shafto Terrace, stated James was standing upright when the brick hit him. Jefferson picked up the brick.

Mrs Walker said James Daglish had been knocked over by the women during the fight and she had warned George, '*Don't throw the brick at the man, you'll kill him with it.*' George had replied, '*I will.*' According to her he ran with the brick until he was four yards from James and then threw it.

When Jefferson approached George and said, '*You have killed the man,*' George picked up another brick, walked a few yards towards Jefferson and then dropped it. Dr Wilson hearing the shouting coming from the back of Shafto Terrace and the sudden silence was sure something awful had happened. He raced to the scene to find James lying prone on the footpath by his back door. The doctor found James had a pulse. He and John Macdonald carried him into his house and the police were alerted. Jefferson then handed the brick to Sergeant Bowser who noted that one edge had grey hair adhering to it.

Once in his home, James stopped breathing and had a feeble heart beat. The doctor administered artificial respiration, but left to collect *'restoratives and instruments'* from his home. On his return, Wilson found his patient close to death. James died within fifteen minutes of the doctor first seeing him.

At 11.30 that morning, Sergeant Bowser charged George Morton with throwing a brick and killing James Daglish. George replied, *'I threw the brick at Frank, but it struck old Jim.'*

At the inquest, led by Mr. Coroner Graham, at the New Inn, Washington, Wilson described James' external injuries as a ' *... contusion over the right cheek bone, a bruise on the bridge of his nose, a small lacerated mark wound on the forehead, and a small incised wound on the crown of his head.'* Apparently ' *... none of these wounds were of any great consequence ...'* but there was also ' *... swelling and discolouration behind the left ear ...'* and '*... marks of bruising and discolouration on the nape of the neck.'*

Wilson went on to report his findings from the post mortem. There was, ' *... a wound on the crown of the head extending to the bone and an extensive blood clot.'* The skull was not fractured. *'The primary cause of death was the shock from the concussion of the brain ...'* and secondly '*... the rupture of some of the arteries of the brain causing pressure on the brain and consequent death.'*

New Washington with the New Inn public house on the right.

He added that a brick thrown with enough force at the base of the neck, could cause a death such as that experienced by James Daglish.

At the Durham winter assizes, which sat in front of Mr Justice Grove, George Morton pleaded guilty to ' *... killing and slaying James Daglish ...'* Mr Blackwell pleaded for the defence that George had aimed the brick at Francis Daglish not James. George was trying to defend his mother who had been on the ground whilst James was *'ill using'* her and Francis had raised the poker to *'strike'* her.

Mr Mulvain, the prosecutor said George was within 4-5 yards of James when he threw the brick. *'The fact of the manslaughter having been committed was not altered by the prisoner throwing the brick at the person who had a poker in hand.'*

Mr Justice Grove observed ' *... it implied that the brick was intended for one person, and struck another who was doing no harm. His Lordship, in passing sentence, said the prisoner had pleaded guilty to a very serious offence, and had the brick been intended to strike the deceased the sentence would have been much more severe.'*

George Morton was ' *... sentenced to six months imprisonment, with hard labour.'*

(*'Newcastle Courant', January 4th, 1878, p.1-2 and January 25th, 1878*).

Today when murders remain unsolved they are called Cold Cases. Here are some very cold cases from the past.

Very Cold Cases

Who did Diane Armstrong upset?

Body found in Tyne
1764

Diane Armstrong was one of two maids who worked for James Oliphant and his wife, Mary. Armstrong's body was found in the Tyne. The Oliphants and remaining servant, Mary Shuttleton, were accused of strangling Armstrong with a rope and throwing her out of a cellar window into the river. They were found not guilty, so who killed her?

The Tyne at Newcastle in the mid 18th century.

In 1815 a reward was offered for evidence associated with a certain crime. This left room for many, including a seaman to attempt to subvert the justice system to win ill gotten gains.

Young Murder
August 28th, 1815

Miss Smith, later Lady Peat, must have thought herself fortunate she was not home in Herrington, County Durham on the night of August 28th, 1815 and the early morning of the 29th. Her servant, Isabella Young, was found murdered with two wounds on the back of her head and a large fracture at the front. She was lying almost naked in a passage leading from the kitchen. The house was then set on fire and the alarm was only raised at about 2 am on the 29th.

On August 13th, 1819 at the Durham assizes, John Eden, James Wolfe, and his son George Wolfe were put on trial for murder, burglary and arson at Herrington. The court took nine hours to find Wolfe and Eden guilty. They were sentenced to be hanged on August 16th.

Members of the Society of Friends (Quakers) inquired into the case and discovered Wolfe had an alibi which placed him a hundred miles from Herrington at the time of the murder. He received a free pardon on September 26th.

Eden insisted he was also innocent so Wolfe persuaded the society to investigate Eden's case. They found a Sunderland seaman, James Lincoln, who was probably interested in the reward, had lied about Eden's involvement. Lincoln was tried at the Durham summer assizes on August 4th, 1820 and found guilty of wilful and corrupt perjury, but who murdered Isabella Young?

Living on your own may be lonely, but it can also be fatal.

Murder Most Foul
January 3rd, 1826

Joe the Quilter was well known and well liked. He lived on his own in a cottage in Homer's-lane, near Warden, Northumberland and was found dead with forty-four wounds on his body. A reward of £100 guineas was offered by the parish warden for the capture of the murderer. The perpetrator was still at large in 1832.

A woman living on her own was perhaps particularly vulnerable.

Body in River Skerne
January 5th, 1840

Susan Dagley had worked at Messrs Pease' Mill for nine months. She had not been seen at her lodgings for five weeks.

Mr Rutter and Mr John Chisman were walking along the River Skerne, a couple of miles from Blackwell Mill, and were on their way to Darlington. They stopped when they spotted a body in the water. It was Dagley. It was clear she had been murdered, but the murderer was never found.

Occasionally a murder case is more complicated.

A Man with a Cause
October 10th, 1869

It was only 24 years since the Irish Famine. Owen Hanlon was in his late twenties and lived in Darlington. According to the newspapers of the time he was a puddler and a known Fenian leader in the North of England. As a puddler he would have stirred molten iron with rods to make malleable wrought iron. As a Fenian leader he led two anti-British fraternal organisations: the Irish Republican Brotherhood (IRB) and the Fenian Brotherhood fighting for the right to an independent Irish Republic. It is not surprising that he was in trouble with the police.

On Sunday evening, October 10th 1869, O'Hanlon was charged at Darlington Police Court with, ' *... attempting to discharge fire-arms with intent to murder Police Constable John Dunn ...*' Dunn, Sergeant Caisley and several other officers had been on duty near Costello's beer house in Haughton Lane. They noted two strange men whispering to each other outside the house. One entered the beer house. The policemen waited outside for a minute and O'Hanlon came out. He went between the policemen, muttered '*You – '* and walked towards the west corner of the house. The police

Darlington in the mid 19th century.

21

followed him and O'Hanlon responded by turning and pointing a revolver at Dunn. According to the police, O'Hanlon was overpowered and prevented from firing the weapon because Caisley seized his arm and Dunn's finger stopped the movement of the hammer. The revolver contained ball cartridges in ' ... *three successive chambers ...*' (*'Leeds Mercury' October 16th, 1869.*)

PC Dunn then revealed to the court that his life had been threatened numerous times and gave an example. Apparently that August he had been walking under a railway bridge. A man had fired at him from the top of the bridge, but missed. Fearing for his life, Dunn had run away. Dunn stated some years ago he had taken in O'Hanlon and a man called McConville for questioning and they had been tried over the murder of Philip Trainer. O'Hanlon had been imprisoned for twelve months. Dunn thought O'Hanlon had threatened him because of this. He inferred it had been O'Hanlon on the bridge.

O'Hanlon was tried for the attempted murder of PC Dunn at Durham Assizes before Justice Lush, High Sheriff Thomas O. Thompson Esq and Under Sheriff G.S. Ransom, Esq. The jury did not even retire before finding O'Hanlon guilty. He was sentenced to twelve months imprisonment and that should have been the end of it.

The Old Town Hall and Shambles, Darlington in the 1860s.

'Newcastle Courant', October 18th, 1872
Approximately three years later O'Hanlon died in suspicious circumstances and the case was heard before a Grand Jury. This is what happened according to witnesses.

O'Hanlon and his friends met to finalise arrangements for his going to America. Unfortunately *'a dispute occurred'* and a *'severe fight'* began between O'Hanlon and another Irishman John Sweeney. Sergeant Cuthbert and PC Watson took a drunken O'Hanlon *'into custody'*. O'Hanlon tried to escape, but a policeman put out his foot and tripped him and O'Hanlon fell heavily to the ground. He walked to the police station without complaining, but was ill the following day. Though he received medical help, within two days his condition had deteriorated to such an extent he was sent home. His father was reported as saying, *'They have finished thee at last.'* O'Hanlon's reply was, *'If I die it is the police who have done it.'* O'Hanlon died. The Grand Jury listened to the evidence, but it was not the policeman who *'tripped'* O'Hanlon who was *'remanded by borough magistrates on a charge of manslaughter'* but Sweeney.

'Leeds Mercury', October 25th, 1872
O'Hanlon's relatives were convinced he had died from police violence. However, O'Hanlon *had* fought with Sweeney. There was evidence of sharp stones in the field where the fight had taken place. O'Hanlon had also been knocked down several times. The post mortem revealed ' ... *the ligature holding the first cervical vertebrae was snapped and an effusion of blood in the head ... may have been caused by a policeman's truncheon.*' It was believed Mr Bignall would, on behalf of O'Hanlon's relatives, open a case against the police.

In a further inquest lasting eight days and recorded in the 'Leeds Mercury' November 22nd, 1872 it was ascertained that *'O'Hanlon had died from effusion of blood on the brain, caused by a blow or through the rupture of the cervical vertebrae.'*

Money was collected by O'Hanlon's friends so they could prosecute the case.

'Witnesses were brought forward who swore they saw PC Cuthbert seriously assault the man with his staff ... On the part of the police this was contradicted by independent evidence.' The jury, despite deliberating for several hours, could not agree a verdict.

At O'Hanlon's funeral, *'Fenians assembled from all parts, and there was the most exciting demonstration against the police.'*

'Leeds Mercury', November 27th, 1872' & 'Newcastle Courant', November 29th, 1872
After the inquest Sweeney was released as the jury could not come to a verdict so *'it was deemed desirable not to carry the case further.'* Mr Bagnal who appeared for Sweeney and probably felt it was the police who should have been prosecuted, *'objected to the case being left open in this manner. Mr Stevenson on behalf of the police said that unless there was more evidence the case would not be pursued further.'* Mr Bagnal *' ... had a prolonged interview with the magistrates, the nature of which did not transpire.'* O'Hanlon's mother was extremely unhappy at the decision. She threatened Thomas Swann, a witness in the coroner's inquiry by saying, *'I will see you are put right before this day a twelvemonth.'*

'Northern Echo', January 27th, 1873
Remnants of the case rumbled on in the Court of Criminal Appeal concerning the inquest on October 11th, 1872 into O'Hanlon's death. Apparently John Johnson, a witness at this inquest held by deputy coroner Thomas Dean, had been found guilty of perjury at the previous Winter Assizes in County Durham. It was put forward that Johnson's conviction should not stand as the coroner was absent and did not appear as ill as he stated. The conviction was upheld. Johnson was refused bail and imprisoned for eighteen months. O'Hanlon was at last allowed to rest in peace, though the perpetrator of the crime was never brought to justice.

Duelling was an organised form of fighting amongst upper class males. It was, of course, illegal.

Duels

Duels of honour were imported from Europe to Britain and condemned and banned from the 17th century. Yet they carried on, though duellists ran the risk of being charged with murder and their seconds, who were responsible for fair play, as accomplices. If caught they would have all been hanged.

Gallants were not deterred and duelling was tolerated by most of the general public. It continued and even flourished in the 18th century. Between the years 1760-1820, 172 duels were fought, 69 men died and 96 were wounded. The perversely titled book the 'Twenty-six Commandments' outlining the rules of duelling etiquette, was published in Ireland in 1777 and probably gave duelling an aura of respectability.

By the late 18th century pistols took the place of swords. These early weapons were not very accurate, but if a ball struck an opponent, it was more likely to kill. There were a mere eighteen trials involving duellists in George III's reign. A reason for this may have been because duels were even fought by Prime Ministers such as Charles James Fox and William Pitt the Younger.

So it comes as no surprise that bloods from important families in the next three accounts also participated in duelling.

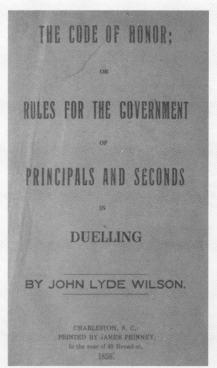

'The Code of Honor' – a rule book for duelling published in 1838 by John Lyde Wilson, former Governor of South Carolina.

Duelling Riddell
August 12th, 1723

'At the assizes, at Newcastle, Mr Edward Riddell, attorney, was tried for killing Captain Lilliburn in a duel, in the Nun's garden, in that town, and acquitted, no proof being made that Mr Riddell killed him.' (Sykes, Vol. I, p. 140.)

Soldiers involved in matters of honour also conducted duels to settle matters, not that the army agreed with their conduct.

Melvil vs Reynolds
January 11th, 1747

As officers in Cholmondley's regiment, Lieutenant Melvil and Ensign Reynolds were quartered in Newcastle. The men were drinking with friends in a local tavern. Despite knowing Melvil was a Scotsman, Reynolds drank and damned all Scotsmen a number of times. Melvil took exception to this, but was restrained by his friends. Both men appear to have been reconciled, but as a precaution their swords were confiscated and the men were placed under arrest at their lodgings.

The following morning Reynolds sent a challenge to Melvil. Reynolds was so impatient he set off for Melvil's lodgings on the east side of Pilgrim Street before he received a reply. Melvil was still in bed, but got dressed and Reynolds was told to go up and see him. Within minutes pistol shots were heard and Reynolds fell to the floor. Reynold's shot had hit the wall above his opponent's head, but Melvil's pistol ball had entered the front of Reynold's chest and exited through his back. Melvil immediately sent for a surgeon, but Reynolds died before help arrived. The inquest took several hours and the coroner's verdict was manslaughter.

Gentlemen were still duelling well into the 19th century as we can see by what took place in the North East on two occasions on different dates.

Pilgrim Street, Newcastle.

Bamburgh Beach
July 1st, 1826

The beach at Bamburgh had probably never staged an event like it: a duel between Thomas Wentworth Beaumont, Esq and John George Lambton, Esq, MP for Durham. They each took a shot at the other and presumably missed. The seconds agreed honour had been satisfied and the men peacefully dispersed.

I suspect when Mr Braddyll entered politics he never thought he would be placing his life in danger. He was not a man to be taken lightly. Perhaps he felt maligned or just had a quick temper. Whatever the reason, Braddyll, a candidate for the Northern Division of Durham, had a very busy morning.

A modern photograph of Bamburgh Castle and the beach where the duel took place.

One Man and Two Duels
September 27th, 1832

At 7 am Braddyll was involved in a duel with Mr Russell Bowlby, a candidate for South Shields. Apparently Braddyll was offended by expressions used by Bowlby in a speech at South Shields. Braddyll wisely decided to have as a second his GP, Mr Irvine, Esq, whilst his antagonist chose Captain Bowlby, presumably a relation. Bowlby was the first to shoot, followed by Braddyll '*discharging his pistol into the air.*' Bowlby, probably grateful his life had been spared, immediately apologised about the tone he had used when commenting on what Braddyll had said. They both then left.

At noon Braddyll was involved in his second duel of the day with a rival candidate for the Northern Division of County Durham, Sir Hedworth Williamson, baronet. This came about because of '*expressions used in speeches about each other*'.

Braddyll's second was William John Banks, Esq, MP and Hedworth's, John Fawcett, Esq. Each man fired two shots at the other. Undoubtedly deciding discretion was the better part of valour, Hedworth and his second agreed he should write the following:

'*I am sorry to have used a term which has been offensive to Mr Braddyll's feelings, and which has been received in a sense in which I never intended it.*'

The parties shook hands and left the field. Braddyll kept his head, his life and won the day! (*Sykes, Vol II, Addendum, p. 398.*)

South Shields Market Place at the beginning of the 19th century.

25

Section Two – Mystery

A mystery encompasses those things that cannot be explained or scientifically proven, rock art for example, or cup and ring marks or henges. Tales of strange happenings make us wonder and the idea of the supernatural, ghosts and haunted places may frighten us, but they can fascinate as well.

Rock Art

Over the centuries the North East has been invaded by Vikings, Scots, Romans and Normans and they have all left their mark on our culture, traditions, religion and landscape. Some are obvious like Hadrian's Wall, others are less so. In the examples below, even the weather has had a hand.

Rock Faces

This face on the right, probably carved into rock by the elements, was found on a gravestone in a churchyard at Byewell.

There are also deliberate marks carved into stone. Our problem is trying to interpret them.

Churchyard at Byewell, Northumberland.

Cup and Ring Marks

Cup and ring marks are mysterious rock engravings made by man and have been documented for over 200 years. There are a lot of them particularly in Northumberland, Durham and Yorkshire, with a few clusters in Derbyshire, Cumbria, Wales and the Isle of Man.

One stone at Lordenshaw, Northumberland has cryptic cup and ring marks as do Hunterheugh Crags, 7 km north-west of Alnwick on the Fell Sandstone escarpment, Dod Law, the North Plantation site at Fowberry and West Horton in Northumberland.

So what are they? Why are they there? Archaeologists appear to think the first carvings are from well before the Early Bronze Age into the Neolithic period. One theory is that they make a statement about the landscape.

There are other stones, however, which stand upright, usually on hill tops. Is there anything in our landscape more intriguing? We wonder how the stones got there, where they came from and their significance.

Left: Lordenshaw Hill, Simonside.

Stone Circles

The traditional name for a stone circle is a henge as in Stone Henge. The word henge comes from Old English meaning stan or 'stone' and partly from 'hengan' meaning hanging. Put the two words together and you have hanging stones.

Many henges have standing stones, but not all. The centre of a henge is usually flat and surrounded by a bank and non-defensive ditch creating a prehistoric earthwork. 180,000 years ago, in the last Ice Age, North East England would have been uninhabited. The Old Stone Age stretching from man's beginnings to about 10,000 BC is divided into Lower, Middle and Palaeolithic periods. When the ice melted Palaeolithic settlers arrived and cave men existed during this period.

Later inhabitants changed their environment by burning charcoal and erecting stone circles. It is believed they were built by Mesolithic hunter-gatherers or perhaps Neolithic farmers, who planted crops, but there is a lot of conjecture about their use. A research team from the Royal College of Art have recently suggested that stones, like those at Stonehenge, can be played as if they are a musical instrument. When struck they 'sing'.

The stones known as Long Meg and her Daughters, Penrith.

Northumberland

At the time of the hunter gatherers, there were 12 henges in Northumberland.

An example of a single standing stone is Bendor Stone also known as Battle Stone (because of the Battle of Homildon Hill in 1402), near Wooler and the village of Akeld. The stone is about 1.8 m tall and is probably Bronze Age.

It stands in a field to the north of Homildon or what is now called Humbleton Hill. Humbleton and Harehope Hills have several prehistoric settlements and forts nestled in the Cheviots and the Northumberland National Park.

Duddo Five Stones or 'Four Stones' or 'The Women' or 'The Singing Stones'

Duddo's Bronze Age sandstone circle is over 400 years old. Almost 10m (32 ft) in diameter, it stands in a prominent position on a hill in farmland and you need permission to visit. The tallest stone is 2.3 m (approximately 10 ft) high and has cup marks, the smallest about 1.5 m high. Some stones have cup marks caused by wind and weather and deep vertical gashes running from top to bottom. However, the bases have been worked by man.

In the 19th century the circle was known as Four Stones until 1903 when one was re-erected. Do the words 'The Women' refer to the stones' 'waists' and does 'The Singing Stones' describe the haunting sound of the wind swirling round the stones? No one knows.

Duddo Four Stones in the 19th century.

In 2008 50% of the circle was excavated. Amongst artefacts like burnt bone coins and gem stones, two stone holes were also found.

The Hethpool Stone Circle

The stones stand in College Valley with Newton Tors towering above them. Some people believe there are two interlinked circles here. If this the case, they are unique in Northumberland. Though much destroyed by farming, the southern circle's diameter is 66 x 50 m and is the best preserved. Eight stones can just be seen above the soil. Four are lying and one which is 1.5 m in height is leaning. There is a sixth stone near the road. The north circle, which is 47 m in diameter, seems to consist of six stones which are above ground.

The Millfield Henges

The Millfield Basin is situated near the parishes of Akeld and Ewart in North Northumberland. The Basin was once filled by Lake Ewart and is near the Rivers Glen and Till. Signs of Mesolithic activity have been found in the form of small tools such as arrow tips made of flint and chert (a similar stone to flint).

Hethpool Stones, College Valley, Northumberland.

The Millfield Henges lie on edge of Millfield Basin and are possibly linked to a drove road (routes along which livestock was driven). They consist of Bronze Age Millfield South Henge, Millfield North Henge, and Whitfield Hill Henge. Archaeologists discovered a cup and marked stone in a pit in the centre of a round ditch at the Millfield South Henge. Thirty pits thought to have supported thirty wooden posts have been excavated here. Cropmarks are all that is left of the Whitfield Hill Henge site. A circular ditch enclosing burial pits and a number of circular enclosures have been discovered at this site.

Three Stone Burn or Iderton Stone Circle, near Alnwick

Three Stone Burn stands where two streams meet. Hedehop Hill and Tathey Crags are nearby. There are 13 pink granite stones visible, though rumours say there were originally 11 or even 16. It was apparently foretold that when the 12th stone was found the discoverer would be rewarded with a fortune. Someone found the 12th and 13th stone, but no money. There may be a spiritual link to a cairn that can be seen whilst journeying to Dod Hill, 1 km to the east.

Durham

What appears to be a really important Neolithic henge was discovered in 2007 whilst excavating a panoramic site for a water reservoir, close to Durham Cathedral.

It is not a settlement or a defensive structure and may have been a place for spiritual activities. Could Durham have been a sacred place for worship, before the cathedral was built? Features which are possibly circular henges or barrows suggest houses for the dead or some sort of ceremonial purpose. Archaeologists have unearthed what are thought to be three raised henges, three manmade ditches, a number of timber stakes cut by bronze tools, pottery and tools such as skin scrapers, and flint knives from approximately 3000 BC.

It is quite a puzzle, because what has been found is not well preserved and experts can only make educated guesses about why and how the site was used.

Surely the mystique of 'cup and circle' marks and stone circles is that they raise more questions than answers. A similar point could be made about some graves.

Grave Tales

Occasionally bodies were buried and forgotten so when skeletons were found centuries later their identity was not known.

Dust to Dust
1272

Greatham, County Durham had a hospital which was founded in 1272, but by 1788 the chapel had become a ruin. A wooden figure on a marble slab lay under an arch that had to be demolished. The tomb was excavated and a stone coffin found. Inside was a skeleton. A lead or pewter chalice was to his left as if it had fallen from his hand. There were also remnants of shoes or sandals. Were these the remains of an important religious figure who was a forerunner of doctors as we know them today?

It was usual for most people to be buried in consecrated ground, but this was not the case for John Richardson.

Garden Burial
September 28th, 1684

Senior tanner, John Richardson, died and was buried in his own garden as he was under sentence of excommunication by the Pope. We do not know what his crime was, but his punishment would have been regarded as dreadful by Roman Catholics in England in the 17th century as it was an act of religious censure. For example Holy Communion would not have been allowed and Richardson would have been ostracised by the religious community in which he lived. The aim was to ensure repentance and a change in unacceptable attitude and behaviour as defined by the Roman Catholic Church. Perhaps Richardson did not repent or did not have time to alter his actions and this is why he was not laid to rest in a churchyard.

The next gravestone lies in Tynemouth Priory and bears the name of Alexander Rollo. Why does it raise questions? Corunna is mentioned.

Alexander Rollo

The inscription reads as follows:

In Memory of
ALEXANDER ROLLO
Late Corporal Royal Artillery
Died May 26th 1856 Aged 82 Years
MARGARET
Wife of the above
Died Oct 4th 1835 Aged 77 Years
CORPORAL ROLLO HELD THE
LANTERN AT THE BURIAL OF
Sir JOHN MOORE
AT CORUNNA ON
17th JANUARY 1809

The inscription informs us that Rollo '*held the lantern at Sir John Moore's funeral at Corunna.*' This begs the questions: who was Sir John Moore and what happened at Corunna?

Rollo's gravestone. (Photograph courtesy of Ewen Windham)

Sir John Moore was regarded as a humane commander and distinguished soldier by the time he was placed in command of the British army in Portugal during the Peninsular War (1808-14). The peninsula was Portugal and Spain and Corunna was a port on the north west tip of Spain. The Battle of Corunna took place on January 16th, 1809,

In 1808 Napoleon Bonaparte was behind an unpopular coup d'etat in Spain. The Spanish rose up and Britain allied itself with Spain against France. Moore was ordered to advance into Spain and attempt to join Spanish forces. He discovered they did not exist and Napoleon thwarted Moore's plans by arriving with 200,000 soldiers. Realising the British army was outnumbered, Moore retreated to Salamanca and then led his men in a skilful fighting retreat to Corunna. Marshal Soult, with 35,000 men, was ordered to pursue Moore's forces.

Sir John Moore.

In their rush to get to get to the coast, discipline broke down as the British regiments of foot laid waste to the villages and countryside through which they passed. The difficult terrain and weather did not help. At Bembibre, two hundred British soldiers were found so drunk in a cellar they were left behind for the French to capture. Moore lost 10,000 men before his exhausted army reached Corunna on January 11th where he expected to find British warships waiting to evacuate his troops. There were no ships.

With Sir David Baird's corps and his own army, Moore had about 35,000 men. Napoleon's army numbered about 153,000.

Moore organised the defence of Corunna whilst also fighting the French so his men could escape by sea once the ships arrived. Amongst other regiments, Alexander Rollo's Royal Artillery, in their blue tunics, were there under the command of Colonel Harding. The Battle of Corunna left the British with 800 casualties and the French with 1,500. Unfortunately, just as victory was almost his, Moore was hit by round shot. Aware of his success, his last words were, '*I hope the people of England will be satisfied! I hope my country will do me justice!*' He was buried in the ramparts of Corunna by the 9th foot.

Charles Wolf's poem 'The Burial of Sir John Moore at Corunna' with its famous line, '*Not a drum was heard, not a funeral note ...*' has in its second verse, a '*lanthorn dimly burning.*' There is a question about the time of day at which Moore's burial took place. However, it is rather nice to think it was possibly Alexander Rollo's hand which held the lantern and that his family was so proud of this fact it was inscribed on his gravestone.

Unexplained events happen all the time. Here are a few.

Strange Stories

How often do we wonder about the origins of a strange place name?

Hell Kettles
1179

There are numerous ideas about the derivation of Hell Kettles which is at Oxenhall, three miles south of Darlington. There are four pits possibly for mining marl (soil or rock containing lime and clay, used as a fertiliser).

One possible explanation could be a reference to some sort of earthquake mentioned in the ' ... *chronicles of Tynemouth and Brompton ...*' Apparently on Christmas Day the earth rose to the height of a tower and stayed like this until evening when it sank making a horrendous noise which terrified everyone in the vicinity. All that was left was a deep pit.

Earthquakes are unusual in the North East, but anyone who was superstitious and saw corpse candles, also known as Jack O' Lantern, Kitty we' the Whisp, Will-of-the-Wisp, Jenny Burn-tail, Spunkie or Joan of the Wood, would have been worried. They were said to be lights emanating from mischievous spirits of the dead, such as stillborn or unbaptized children, darting between heaven and hell and leading travellers astray.

The lights were more likely to be animals or barn owls coated in honey fungus which is luminescent or methane gas produced by rotting organic material in bogs, marshland or even graveyards. However, this was not always the case.

Vault Robberies in 'All Saints'

People in Church Walk, Newcastle often claimed they saw lights in 'All Saints' graveyard. They were thought to be *'corpse candles'*. A watch was set and the mystery was solved. The light was held by a grave robber who was caught carrying spoils from one of the vaults.
(Newcastle Town, Charlton, R.J. p. 194.)

There were claims about objects too, such as the Lee Penny.

Late 18th century, All Saints, Church Walk, Newcastle.

The Lee Penny
September 27th, 1645

There is a story that when the plague came to Newcastle, the inhabitants were so concerned they raised money so they could borrow the Lee Penny from the Lee family.

The stone was said to cure all diseases in man or beast. It was dipped in water which was then used to wash a wound, given as a drink to those bitten by a rabid dog, or to diseased animals. It became so famous that people came from Yorkshire and all parts of Scotland seeking the water in which it had been plunged.

The penny was a dark red stone, triangular in shape and only about a $1/2$ inch in size. It was set in a silver shilling and was marked with a cross dating it possibly in Edward I's reign. The Lee family possessed it from about 1320 and it probably gave them a good income over several centuries. So did the penny heal the sick or was it a trick to gain money from the the ill and dying?

Belief in the supernatural, ignorance and lack of scientific knowledge could lead to belief in the Lee Penny or the accusation of witchcraft.

Who to Blame?
July, 1668

Alice Armstrong was the wife of Shotton labourer Christopher Armstrong. At the Durham Assizes she was tried for *'bewitching to death an oxe belonging to Barbra Thompson. Sentence not recorded.'* (Sykes, Vol II, Addenda, p. 370).

We do not know what happened to Alice, but we do know what happened in the next story.

Newcastle's Icarus
December 7th, 1733

The residents of Bailiff Gate in Newcastle had probably not seen anything like this before! A man flew from the top of the castle and landed safely. He then tied weights to an ass's legs, expecting it to fly as well. Not surprisingly the poor beast plummeted to the ground. The weights bruised some spectators, knocked others down and a girl was killed! There is no record of what happened to the man or the ass.

A story about a prospective flying ass is strange, but Robert Louis Stevenson could not have created a more interesting tale than that of Jeremiah Moore.

Kidnapped
August 20th, 1753

Jeremiah Moore was aged 57 when he died at Norton, near Stockton. According to him his eldest brother had arranged for him to be, *'carried into Turkish slavery'*. Moore escaped from the Turks only to be pressed into the Royal Navy in the Mediterranean. When his eldest brother died, Moore eventually inherited, *'his estate'* and *'converted it into money'*.

Apparently he was good to all his poor neighbours. He had no relatives, but he made Mrs Ann Kendall, his housekeeper, his executrix (female executor of the will) and residuary legatee (person to whom the testator's estate is left after specific bequests have been made). He left £3,000 in trust for her son and £1,500 each to six gentleman who'd, *' … helped him in his adversity …'* They all received their legacies at Moore's house in Norton, *'on the first day of the following March, over a large bowl of punch, and they were yearly to commemorate that day as long as they lived it being the anniversary of the day he escaped slavery.'* (Sykes, Vol. I, p. 206.)

At least Moore received his inheritance and justice was seen to be done. A child, Mr Davison and a sergeant-at-mace in the three tales below also had fortunate endings to their tales.

Child Taken
August 8th, 1763

A three year old child from Shotton Edge, Blagdon strayed some distance from her home. A dog, which was the child's playmate, made obvious signals that the child was on the road to Newcastle. Believing in his dog's instincts, the child's father went in that direction. On his journey, someone told him about a beggar woman and child who were not far ahead. He found both of them. The child was his. The woman was put before Matthew Ridley, Esq. At Blagdon and, *' … was committed to the House of Correction in Morpeth.'* (Sykes, Vol.1, p.242.)

Shotton Edge cottages, Blagdon, Northumberland.

Death That Never Was
January, 1773

Mr Davison from Earsdon was pronounced dead, but because of the absence of any relatives, it was decided the funeral would be delayed for three days. On the second day Davison's supposed corpse showed signs of life. One can only imagine the shock this must have caused.

Left: A row of stone cottages in Earsdon, Northumberland.

Look Before You Ride
February 28th, 1755

Newcastle's Flesh Market would have been full of butchers selling meat during the day. At night it should have been empty and silent. A sergeant-at-mace rode through it one evening and unfortunately did not spot a butcher's hook and caught his jaw on it whilst his horse carried on. The sergeant was left suspended from the hook until someone found him. He recovered despite his wound.

The last three stories had happy endings, but this is one of misfortune in the Robert Louis Stevenson style.

The Flesh Market, seen here in 1820, has its origins in the medieval Cloth Market.

Swan Saga
March 18th, 1786

In 1705 Thomas Swan at nine years of age was, *'trepanned from his father's house, Richard Swann, Esq, of Benwell Hall, near Newcastle.'* This was done to disinherit him.

He was *'put on board the new Britannia brig ...'*, wrecked off the Scilly Isles with Sir Cloudesley Shovel's fleet. *' ... taken by an Algerine vessel, sold into slavery and, after four years imprisonment, was set at liberty by Redeeming Friars. After this he was again taken prisoner. Carried and sold for a slave to a planter at South Carolina, where he suffered almost every human woe.'*

In 1726 he returned to England and a footman and nurse identified him in Newcastle. He tried to claim his inheritance (£20,000 per annum), for twenty five years, but with no relatives or friends who could help, it was in vain.

He eventually settled in North Dalton, Hull and married Jane Cole. He became an alderman, mayor and had a son, William Swan. Thomas died in 1735 and William died, *' ... at an obscure lodging near Chiswell Street, London.'*
(*'The Universal Register'*; Sykes, Vol. I, p. 338.)

The 18th century was the age of the Enlightenment. When rationality and reason would come to the fore, sweeping away superstition, prejudice and religious assertions. There had been advances in medical knowledge in the 17th century such as the discovery of salivary glands and the circulation of the blood and more were to follow in the 18th century. So had enlightenment reached Newcastle at this time?

Mystery Cure: Earth-bathing
July 1791

'Dr Graham, to shew the nature and safety of earth-bathing for the cure of various diseases, had himself, and a young woman, troubled with scorbutic disorder, placed naked in the earth, and covered up to their lips, in Hanover Square, chapel ground, in Newcastle, from twelve o'clock at noon till six in the evening each day. Great numbers attended to see this curious exhibition.' (Sykes, Vol. I, p. 358.)

It is no surprise, perhaps, that crowds were 'enlightened' when they watched two naked individuals earth bathing, just as they gathered to celebrate the downfall of an admiral.

A Political Scapegoat

On first reading the report below, one might assume that Admiral John Byng (1704-57) was a pariah and someone akin to Guy Fawkes.

July 26th, 1796

'The populace of Newcastle honoured Admiral Byng by an effigy, set on an ass, elegantly decorated with proper labels, &c., preceded by a person on a mule, with a white standard, on which was this motto: 'Oh, back your sails, for God's sake! A shot may hit the ship.' On each side of his hat was Bung, and round his waist was, 'This is the villain that would not fight.'

'Having paraded the town, the procession halted at the carrion burning place at the Flesh Market, where a gallows was erected, on which, after being severely treated, he was hung, the prepared funeral pile lighted, and he, with ignominy and reproach, was suffered to perish. At Gateshead, Shields, Sunderland, and other places, this noble admiral was similarly caricatured.' (Sykes, Vol. I, p. 215.)

Byng had an illustrious career in the Royal Navy. This was not to last. After joining the navy at 14 years of age he became Vice-Admiral in 1747 and Admiral of the Blue (the navy was divided into three squadrons in order of seniority Red, White and Blue) on March 17th, 1756.

At the time of Byng's downfall Thomas Pelham-Hooles, 1st Duke of Newcastle was Prime Minister from May 10th, 1754 to November 16th, 1756 followed by William Cavendish, Duke of Devonshire in 1756-57, though the effective premier was Pitt the 'Elder'.

The British Government failed to recognise the strategic military importance of Minorca in controlling the Mediterranean. It was obvious as early as 1755 that the French meant to take the island and yet no action was taken to defend it.

Appointed to command the fleet of 13 ships, Byng found difficulties placed in his way. His protests were ignored and then he was inexplicably delayed waiting for orders. This wait proved critical to the expedition's lack of success. He sailed on April 6th, 1756, just after the French had landed 15,000 soldiers on Minorca's west shore.

Byng decided to return from Minorca if he could not realise his orders and shared this in his correspondence to his superiors. Whilst in Gibraltar, the governor gave him fewer soldiers than he requested. Byng shared his feelings of

Admiral John Byng by Thomas Hudson, 1749.

impending failure with the Admiralty. George II was shown the letter and said, 'This man will not fight!'

On May 20th, 1756 during the Battle of Minorca, Byng ordered his leading ships to engage with the French fleet whilst his flagship and the other ships stayed out of range. The French made off having badly damaged Byng's leading ships. He ignored his flag captain's suggestion to stand out of line so the centre of the French fleet could be brought to closer action. Byng's reasoned that Admiral Matthews had been dismissed many years earlier for doing this.

For the next four days, Byng tried to unsuccessfully to contact the British Fort St Philip on Minorca and also to sight the French. His ships were now almost unserviceable, so he sailed for Gibraltar for repairs and to land his wounded. Once there, reinforcements arrived and he prepared to return and relieve the garrison on Minorca.

French Admiral Galissoniere's dispatch stating that the English: *'made up their minds to sheer off, and did not appear again during the whole of the next day,'* arrived in London before Byng's report and caused uproar when it appeared in British newspapers. The Admiralty and senior politicians had a scapegoat: Byng. Concerned for their positions, First Lord, Admiral Lord Anson, whose father was closely connected to the Duke of Newcastle, and other senior politicians had Byng relieved of command, returned to England and placed in custody.

It was not until June 23rd that Byng's edited account making him seem *'indecisive and cowardly'* appeared in the 'London Gazette', thus allowing his superiors to evade all responsibility. Fort St Philip capitulated on the June 29th. Byng became the public face of failure and the mob chanted, *'Swing, swing Admiral Byng.'*

He was tried by court martial on December 27th, 1756 for breach of the Articles of War, but acquitted of disaffection and cowardice. He was convicted of not trying his best in pursuing the enemy or in battle. The sentence

A political cartoon about Byng.

was death. Parliament and George II were approached in vain attempts to spare Byng's life.

On the March 14th, 1757, 52 year old Byng was shot on the foredeck of his own ship the 'HMS Monarch' by a platoon of Royal Marines and was the only Admiral to be shot for not trying his utmost. The Articles of War were amended 22 years later.

Just as someone's career can fall from dizzy heights, similarly objects may also fall to earth.

Great Balls of Fire
November 11th, 1799

What appeared to be *'great balls of fire'* were first seen to the east of Greatham, Hartlepool and the surrounding area at 5-6 am. They fell in succession till dawn and *'The atmosphere was very clear, and the moon, which was full, shone with uncommon brilliancy.'* The meteors were compared to shooting stars which became stationary and then *'burst'* and went north trailing *'floating fire in various shapes, some point, some radiated, some in sparks, and others in large columns.* Spectators said the sky seemed to open, and to display a number of moving *'luminous serpents'* which broke *'into separate balls, and fell towards the earth in a shower of fire.'* This light show continued for two hours until at eight o'clock lightning appeared.

The whole scene was described as, *'sublimely awful'* by fishermen from Hartlepool who were at sea. (*Sykes, Vol. I, p. 395.*)

Just as there can be amazing sights in the heavens, the rivers and fish have their own strange stories.

Fishy Tales

Waiting for the Boats, Cullercoats Bay.   Auty Series, G.H., N/C., No. 3596.

A postcard of fisherwives waiting for the boats at Cullercoats Bay.

In the 16th century the River Tyne would have been full of salmon.

It has a Ring to It
1559

The descendants of Rev E. Anderson might like to know why his signet ring had a fish engraved on it. Alderman and merchant, Mr Anderson, leant over a bridge at Newcastle and accidentally dropped his ring in the water. He must have thought he had lost it forever, until a servant went to the market some time later and bought a salmon. Inside was his ring!

Salmon are not the only fish found off our shores.

Jaws off our Shores!
September, 1757

Fishermen hauling their nets in the River Tweed, just below the bridge at Berwick, were expecting to catch salmon. What they landed was a six foot, green shark! It thrashed about as they hauled it in it, sending water high into the air and once in the shallows the desperate movements of its tail made a huge hollow in the sand. Some gentleman who had been to both the Indies said it was from the East Indies. They presumed it had followed the East India fleet to the Firth and spotted the salmon in the Tweed. When they slit open its belly they found a clasp knife.

The three bridges at Berwick: the Old Bridge (1611), the Royal Tweed Bridge (1925) and the Royal Border Bridge, a 19th century railway viaduct.

North Sea cod may be off the menu today because of falling stocks, but in the 18th century there was no such problem.

A Cod Fish Tale
February 18th, 1765

I bet when Mr Harbottle from Bedlington bought a cod from Blyth that is all he expected to get. What he found inside the fish was a gold mourning ring with a defaced or worn away inscription.

And just to prove the sighting of sharks off the North East coast was not a one off, read the next two accounts.

Jaws Two!
September 22nd, 1788

Fishermen at Cullercoats caught two sharks almost six feet in length and with two rows of teeth.

Sunderland fishermen were expecting to catch herring in Whitburn Bay. What they caught was a five foot shark.

316. FISHERMEN MENDING NETS, CULLERCOATS

Cullercoats fishermen mending their nets.

Today the River Tyne is regarded as the best in England for salmon numbers, but this was not the case in the 19th and 20th centuries when the river was polluted by industry. This is another account about what a fish will attempt to eat.

I See No Chips!
October 12th, 1825

'A pair of spectacles, in a steel case, were taken out of the maw of a salmon, in the Flesh Market, Newcastle.' (Sykes, vol. II, p. 189.)

Northumberland's Ghosts and Ghouls

Northumberland is England's most northern county. It has been fought over for thousands of years. If there are ghosts, they would have a lot to be unsettled about.

Alnwick Castle

Norman Baron Yve de Vescy first built a timber and motte castle in the 11th century. This was later replaced by a stone castle in the 12th century. Its latest design was created in the 14th century by the Percys.

According to legend a lord and vampire who used to own the land lived under the castle. He attacked villagers at night. Plague was also blamed on him, so the villagers dug him up and burnt him.

Most castles have their tales of ghosts and Bebba's Fort is no exception.

A crucifix etched into the wall of Alnwick Castle.

A lion rampart on Alnwick Castle's walls.

Bebba's Fort

Bebba's Fort or Bamburgh Castle, built on the Whin Sill and situated in a strategic coastal position surveying the frontier between England and Scotland, was probably built in the 6th century. Traditionally thought to have been founded by King Ida, Bebba's Fort was probably named after Ida's grandson's queen.

Apparently two ghosts have made themselves known in the castle. The rattling chains and heavy footsteps of a knight in full armour and the horrific ghostly apparition of a woman swathed in a green cloak as she plummets from the battlements only to disappear in the murk below.

An etching of Bamburgh Castle, once home to the Kings of Northumbria.

Berwick Castle with a keenly fought over defensive position, also deserves to have at least one ghost.

Berwick Castle

The town of Berwick, because of its strategic location at the mouth of the River Tweed, suffered centuries of conflict between the English and Scots and like its castle, changed hands several times. This explains why it has an impressive, mainly Elizabethan bastioned wall encircling it, and can be walked on today.

The castle was built by the Scottish King David I and if you listen carefully you may hear the ghostly swirl of bagpipes from a phantom piper as he walks back and forth along the battlements.

All of Northumberland and Durham lived in fear of attack by the Scottish army. Today, beautiful Blanchland is like the village that time forgot. Unfortunately, the Scots did not forget its existence and events in 1715 also involved the village in treason, intrigue and a daring escape. No wonder there are reports of ghostly sightings.

Blanchland

Blanchland or 'White Land' was named after the white woollen habits worn by the French canons whose 12th century abbey once stood on the site. The present day village was built on top of the Abbey's foundations and with its stones.

An arch, once the entrance to Blanchland Abbey.

The village lies on the Northumberland and Durham border in the Derwent valley close to the River Derwent. It was owned by the Bishop of Durham and then later by Nathaniel Lord Crewe in the early 18th century. Blanchland then became part of a charitable trust when he died.

There is an old tale of the monks being warned about a border raid. A fog descended as the Scottish army crossed Hexhamshire Common. The monks, thinking they were safe and God was on their side, rang their bell in celebration. Unfortunately the army followed the sound of the bell and massacred them all. From that day on, so the tale goes, you can hear the mournful tolling on certain days and ghostly monks can be seen around the churchyard. The monks are reputedly buried in a mass grave in the churchyard.

The Lord Crewe Arms Hotel, Blanchland

The 'Lord Crewe Arms Hotel' formerly the 16th century Abbot's house.

This hotel is medieval in origin and has all the essentials for a 'spooky' stay with its flagged stone floors; low beams; a stone vaulted ceiling; stone walls and a concealed Priest's hole in one of the huge stone fireplaces. It will come as no surprise to learn that three of the bedrooms are apparently haunted.

The most famous ghost is that of Dorothy Forster. Her brother, Thomas, was the Tory MP for Northumberland and Jacobite commander during the 1715 uprising. He surrendered to government forces at Preston and was held in London's Newgate Gaol, but not for very long. Within three days, before a trial for the capital offence of treason, he escaped with the assistance of Dorothy and a bunch of duplicate keys.

His hiding place was the priest's hole at the Lord Crewe Arms, which at the time was owned by the Forster's aunt, Lady Dorothy Crewe, and from there he was safely smuggled to France. Dorothy apparently deceived the authorities into thinking Thomas had died by putting sawdust in a coffin and installing it in the Forster vault in Bamburgh.

It is said that Dorothy haunts the Bamburgh Room at the Lord Crewe Arms and urges visitors to take a message to her brother telling him that it is not safe to return to England. Her ghost has also appeared in the road as she walks towards the public house.

Another ghost is that of a white monk, kneeling at the bottom of a bed in the Radcliffe Room. He appears solid and then just fades from sight.

A flickering light beneath a door has been seen and heavy footsteps and doors opening and closing have been heard by a visitor sleeping in part of the hotel which was supposedly empty and the outside door locked.

Chesters Fort also has stories of phantoms.

Chesters Roman Fort, Chollerford

The fort lies on Hadrian's Wall and was built over 2,000 years ago to guard a bridge over the River Tyne. A Spanish cavalry regiment from Asturias garrisoned it for over 200 years. It is said that 500 phantom Roman cavalrymen, wake and ride out from the strong room in the Roman fort every night.

The remains of the bath house of Chesters Fort, Hadrian's Wall.

Chillingham Castle does not have phantom cavalry, but it does have enough resident ghosts for the whole country.

Chillingham Castle

This castle, first owned by the Earls Grey, is situated in a key defensive position in the border regions in Northumberland. It would have been a wild and desolate place and today there are only a few houses near its gates. Even the name Chillingham seems to hint at its chilling and bloody past.

A tower with a panoramic view was built in the 12th century to make it difficult for the Scottish army to secretly advance across the region. In 1297 the stronghold was attacked by William Wallace who burnt women and children from the Grey family in the monastery. It was not until 1344 that Edward I permitted the building to look like the castle we see today.

During the Wars of the Roses, the Grey family fought on both sides, thus saving the Chillingham estate. Those who fought for the Lancastrians ordered the executions of eight Grey family members and Sir Ralph Grey actually ordered the hanging, drawing and quartering of his own son.

The castle is said to have several ghosts, which is not surprising because of its bloody history and the fact that very few prisoners who entered the castle ever came out. This was probably because of the dungeons and torture chamber which are situated in its depths. Prisoners, many of them Scots, would have had their limbs broken and been thrown down a 21 foot hole. Apparently if you venture to look down the hole, you may see a young female ghost looking back at you.

During renovations to the dungeons, a skeleton was found sitting in a chair, but the bones turned to dust with the rush of air. There is also a secret dungeon or oubliette which is entered by trapdoor. A child's bones were found here.

The torture chamber's floor sloped so that blood and other bodily fluids could flow into a trench at one side. The head torturer was John Sage and apparently the prisoner's screams could be heard in some of the rooms above. The instruments he used are still in place and consisted of man traps, chains, a bed of nails, a boiling pot, leg and branding irons, a spiked seat, thumb screws, an iron maiden and a rack to name a few. It appears the chamber was used for three years and in that time fifty people per week were killed there.

Chillingham Castle in Northumberland has had many Royal visitors which belie its dark past. These include: Henry III, Edward I, James I, Charles I and Edward VIII.

One of the most famous phantoms is the Blue Boy or Radiant Boy who haunts the Pink Room. His moans and cries at midnight come from a corridor cut into a 10 foot wall leading to another tower and have woken sleeping guests. Dressed in blue and surrounded by light, he has been known to have approached those he has awakened in their bed. His clothes date from the Restoration period when Charles II was on the throne.

Interestingly, a young boy's bones with fragments of blue material and a man's skeleton were discovered in this room in the 1920s. They were found lying close to a trapdoor leading to vaults below in a wall where a fireplace is now. Once his bones were placed in consecrated ground, the blue boy was never seen again.

A very pale, frail woman is supposed to haunt the pantry. A footman, who had retired to bed for the night, reported being asked by a woman for some water. He started to get it for her when he realised no one could have entered the room because it was locked. When he turned, there was no one there.

A maid was said to have fled from a room in the middle of the night and refused to return. It was discovered a cook had committed suicide here at one point in the castle's history.

The Edward Room, named after Edward I, lies high up in the castle above the dungeons and torture chamber below. There seems to be a strange atmosphere here and whispering, foul smells and a swinging chandelier have all been recorded.

Poor, lonely, Lady Mary Berkley also known as the Ghost of the Portrait, or the Grey Lady, supposedly wanders the corridors leaving an icy chill behind her. She was married with a small child when her husband left her to live with her sister, Lady Henrietta.

Mary's portrait used to hang in the nursery, but it was soon removed elsewhere when children and maids complained that she stepped out of the portrait and followed them.

If you decide to visit the 'chillingly' named Devil's Walk, in the castle grounds be prepared to encounter a few troubled phantoms. Apparently it was once strewn with Scottish corpses which were left till only bones remained to deter any other would be attackers.

John Sage, the head torturer, was also hanged from one of the trees here. Apparently he accidentally killed his girlfriend.

The medieval courtyard of Chillingham Castle.

Her relatives and friends got their revenge by cutting pieces off him as he was dying.

If you step into the garden for a quiet stroll, it is rumoured you might meet a ghostly funeral procession. The courtyard will not give you much relief as there are phantoms reputed to haunt here as well.

Also be careful if you head for the lake. Corpses from the dungeons were dumped here and there have been tales of at least one ghost and strange noises emanating from this spot.

Ghosts are not always the victims of torture. Craster Tower also has many reports of supernatural sounds and sightings.

Craster Tower

Craster Tower, originally a 14th century pele tower built by Sir Edmund Craster, is situated in Craster, Northumberland. The tower had a main entrance on the first floor and had four floors. It is now part of a Grade II 18th century country house and has been owned by the Craster family for over 800 years.

The land of Crawcestre was purchased in the 12th century by Albert, possibly from the Rhineland, who married Christina from Redcar, Yorkshire. He built a hall he named 'Crawe' which is old English for crow. Not surprisingly, by the 15th century the difficult to pronounce Crawcestre had been shortened to Craster.

There are reports of several ghosts. Apparently you can hear the sounds of swords ringing out in a ghostly duel and the wheels of a phantom coach. Furniture in the house has also been moved. The spectre of a grey lady also walks from the front door and upstairs to the drawing room. She also haunts one bedroom and apparently has been known to ensure that children are tucked in at night.

Craster Tower's walls are built of squared ashlar (finely dressed stone) and are about 2 m thick at basement level.

A lady also haunts Dilston Hall.

Dilston Hall

The original 15th century tower house was incorporated into the Dilston Hall's west wing. The hall lies between Corbridge and Hexham. The ruins of Dilston Hall and its chapel are a poignant reminder of its last owner, the tragic 3rd Earl of Derwentwater. He was executed for his role in the Stuart uprising of 1715 and his estates were confiscated by the crown. He is not the only interesting member of the Catholic Radcliffe family to have lived in the hall. His brother Charles also fought in the 1715 rebellion. He was captured, escaped abroad but became embroiled in the 1745 rebellion. On his return to England, he was captured and also executed.

Lady Derwentwater's phantom has been seen in two places. First walking in the woods and secondly looking out of a window in the hall as if waiting for her husband's return.

Reports of mists and lights have been recorded in the castle. Apparitions have been seen on the Lord's Bridge at night as well as the sound of a horse's hooves. Could they belong to James Radcliffe's steed as he was also known as the 'Galloping Lord'?

The chapel is possibly the most haunted of all. Banging noises have been heard emanating from the crypt and there has been poltergeist activity here.

Phantoms at Featherstone Castle take part in a tragic love story which they play out every year at the same time.

Featherstone Castle

The castle is now a private residence about two miles south of Haltwhistle. It played a key role in battles between the English and Scottish armies. It is situated in a defensive position close to where Hartley Burn meets the River South Tyne. It was originally a 12th century tower and in the 14th century a pele tower was added. In the 19th century a Gothic mansion was built. It is Grade I listed and linked to a tragic love story. Rather like Romeo and Juliet, two young people fell in love, were thwarted and suffered a harrowing end. Except this tale is not set in Verona, nor apparently is it fiction.

Featherstone Castle's first owner was Helias de Featherstone. Part of the barony of Langley, the manor was ruled by Scotland.

This is a Northumbrian love story about Abigail Featherstonehaugh and her lover a local Ridley man. Unfortunately, Abigail was expected to marry a Baron's son and the wedding was agreed. The bride, groom and their guests went hunting as part of the marriage celebrations. Her incensed lover, attacked the wedding party and the groom fought back. The result was that they were all killed.

However, that evening on the stroke of midnight, the sound of horses' hooves were heard, the banqueting hall door opened and Abigail led in the ghostly wedding party. The Baron fainted at seeing the blood stained procession. Apparently the party can also be seen annually on January 17th across the river from the castle in a valley called Pynkin's Cleugh.

An unfortunate ghost is supposed to haunt Haughton Castle.

Haughton Castle

The castle is a privately owned Grade I listed mansion, north of Humshaugh in Northumberland. Ranulf de Haughton possibly built the first storey of this 13th century property. Owned by George Widdrington in 1260 as a tower house, it was enlarged and fortified in the 14th century. In the 16th century it was attacked by reivers who undoubtedly knew it had fallen into a state of disrepair.

The ghost of Archie Armstrong is supposed to haunt this castle which was first fortified in the 1373. Sir John Widdrington had to go to a meeting in York. Before he left, Armstrong, a reiver, was caught rustling cattle and placed in the castle dungeon.

After a two day ride Widdrington discovered the dungeon's key in his pocket and realised he had forgotten to mention Armstrong's welfare to anyone. When Widdrington returned he was told tales of the prisoner's cries. On opening the dungeon Armstrong was found to be dead.

Armstrong's supposed moans frightened those who heard him so much, that the Rector of Simonburn was requested to exorcise the ghost. It worked – for a time. When the Bible used for the exorcism was sent to London to be rebound, the ghost returned.

Ghosts have not only been reported on our mainland, but also in a lighthouse on the Farne Isles.

Longstone Lighthouse, Farne Isles.

Two keepers of Longstone's lighthouse in 1976 claimed they could hear Grace Horsley Darling's footsteps in the engine room. As she had been dead for well over a century it is interesting to recall the events that took place which might have made her spirit return to its childhood haunts.

Grace was the 22 year old daughter of William and Thomasina Darling and the seventh child of nine. In 1838 William was the keeper of the Longstone Lighthouse on Longstone Rock, one of the Outer Staple Islands of the Farne Islands, off the coast of Northumberland.

A light had been requested here as far back as the late 17th century by Sir John Clayton and in 1755 by Captain J. Blackett, but the authorities turned them down. The Elder Brethren of Trinity House could not agree about the maintenance costs of the light. It was finally designed and built by Joseph Nelson in 1826. The red and white lighthouse was initially called the Outer Farne lighthouse.

An illustration showing Grace Darling, her father William, the Longstone Lighthouse. and the rescue of the crew of the 'SS Forfarshire'.

On September 5th, 1838 the paddle steamer the 'SS Forfarshire', was carrying a mixed cargo and sixty passengers when she sailed from Hull on her way to Dundee.

On September 6th the 'Forfarshire' developed a leaking boiler, the engine stopped and she drifted off the black rocks of the Farne Islands in the middle of a terrible storm. At 4 am she struck Big Harcar Rock and by 4.15, the steamer had broken in two. Eight of the crew and one passenger managed to fling themselves into one of the ship's lifeboats and were picked up by a sloop, the 'Montrose', but 48 people went down with the stern of the ship.

The wreck was spotted by Grace at 4.45 am, but it was not till 7 am that moving figures were seen on the rock. Conditions were so poor that William Darling felt the North Sunderland lifeboat would not be able to launch.

Grace and her father set off to rescue the survivors in a 21ft open rowing boat called a coble. They rowed for a mile in high seas. Whilst William went on to the rock and found eight men, one who was badly injured and one woman holding two dead children, Grace kept the coble from being wrecked on the reef by rowing backwards and forwards. William and three of the rescued men rowed Grace, the woman and the injured man back to the lighthouse. Grace's father then returned with two of the Forfarshire crew and rescued four more men.

Grace was sent £50 by Queen Victoria and both she and her father were awarded gold medals from the Royal Humane Society and silver medals from the National Institution for the Preservation of Life from Shipwreck (now the RNLI). She became a reluctant heroine in Victorian England, but unfortunately died of tuberculosis on October 20th, 1842.

Grace Darling is the only ghost said to haunt Longstone Lighthouse, but inns, with their continually changing population, have also reported ghostly activity. The Paranormal Society have declared the Schooner Hotel in Alnmouth, Northumberland to be the most haunted in the county.

The Grace Darling Memorial, Bamburgh.

The Schooner Hotel, Alnmouth

Built in the 17th century as an unassuming coaching inn, it was at the centre of life in the port of Alnmouth and has a secret past. It was the haunt of smugglers who may have found the underground tunnels linking the cellar to the port rather useful.

This Grade II listed building is nestled amongst fishermen's cottages and granaries in an idyllic setting. Do not be fooled. There are 32 rooms in the inn and supernatural activity has been reported in each one. In fact sixty or more ghosts are said to haunt the Schooner Hotel.

The centre of paranormal activity appears to be Room 28. There have been reports of people feeling terrified and sensing a presence in this room. Murders or suicides may explain the sound of women's screams and the haunting cries and voices of children. Bangs, knocks, whispers and feelings of dread, sickness and dizziness have all been experienced in Rooms 29 and 30. A phantom was seen running from Room 20, hitting the fire doors and turning at which point the terrified staff fled. Rooms 16 and 17 have a connecting door which is hidden from all but the staff and numerous apparitions have been sighted standing at the bottom of beds in these rooms.

One ghost prowling the corridors is said to be a young boy responsible for waking visitors by knocking on their doors. Other phantoms are a soldier who walks backwards and forwards and a maid who appears on the stairs.

Other hotels have stories of ghosts haunting their premises.

The Tynemouth Lodge Hotel

A House of Correction was built here in 1789 and the Tynemouth Lodge Hotel was erected next door for Mr William Hooper in 1799. Hooper ran the hotel for a number of years. It consisted of three floors and was linked to the House of Correction (a prison for minor offenders on their way to Morpeth Gaol) and the Justices Room (a Court House) by a tunnel leading from the hotel cellar which was once a kitchen providing food for prisoners. The judges stayed at the hotel whilst conducting their business in the Court House.

CORRECTION HOUSE BANK

Perhaps because of the contrasting nature of the clientele in the hotel and the Correction House there are reports of ghosts. However, these phantoms are not what you might have expected. Successive tenants in the first floor flat above the public house have reported children being chased by a lady in the early hours of the morning.

The Schooner Hotel, Alnmouth.

The windows of the former Correction House.

The Tynemouth Lodge Hotel, North Shields.

Newcastle also has many tales of phantoms.

46

Newcastle Spooks

One has to climb Dog Leap Stairs to appreciate its history and height. It is not difficult to imagine apparitions or ghostly sounds here.

Dog Leap Stairs

In the early 1700s, the story of Bessie Surtees, daughter of a Newcastle banker and her elopement with John Scott, the son of a coal merchant, must have shocked all of Newcastle.

After escaping through a window of her house in Sandhill, Bessie fled on John's horse with her family in pursuit. In desperation they supposedly rode up Dog Leap Stairs, which are almost impossibly steep. John and Bessie made it to the top, her family did not. Apparently the sound of ghostly horses and their hooves stopping half way up the stairs can often be heard. The couple married in Scotland and John, despite his humble origins, became the first Earl of Eldon and Lord Chancellor of Great Britain.

Right: Bessie Surtees' house is two 16th/17th merchant houses, 41 and 44 Sandhill.

In the past, Scots were not liked in Newcastle because of the border wars and numerous attempts to lay siege and storm the city's walls. They succeeded in gaining entry in the 17th century which would not have increased their popularity so the 1715 and 1745 Jacobite rebellions would only have made the inhabitants of Newcastle even more wary.

The Bigg Market Ghost
1752

Ewan McDonald (see 'Crime and Punishment', Gallows Walk, p. 29) because of taunts about his Scottish nationality used his fists and killed a man. McDonald was hanged for his crime and his ghost supposedly haunts the Bigg Market. They say he is often seen in the Pig and Whistle or further up the street.

Left: The Bigg Market, Newcastle's oldest market.

The next haunting occurs in a churchyard.

The Graveyard Ghost

There are several variations of this tale. The girl was the daughter of a rich landowner. She fell in love with a young priest and used to meet him close to the 12th century St Andrew's Churchyard in Newcastle. One night he thought he saw her running away from him between the gravestones and then she disappeared. The next morning he learned that she had died at the exact time he saw her in the churchyard.

Left: Newcastle's city walls near the 12th century St Andrew's Church.

Cathedrals, like churchyards have their fair share of ghostly sightings.

Knight Walks

St Nicholas Cathedral, near Amen Corner in Newcastle, was formerly a church dating back to the 12th century. The lurking phantom of a knight in armour has been seen and the sound of clanking metal heard in the cathedral. His favourite spot appears to be near the stone resting place of an unknown knight from the 13th century.

Centuries before this the Romans occupied Newcastle.

The Roman Spectre

The Romans built their bridge Pons Aurelius across the Tyne and the name transferred to their fort which is now Newcastle. The fort formed part of the Roman Wall.

Apparently a ghostly Roman soldier has been seen outside the castle walls.

Right: The remains of Hadrian's Wall at West Denton, Newcastle in the 1950s.

County Durham's Phantoms

County Durham, Land of the Prince Bishops, lies with Northumberland to the north and Cumbria to the west. Pre-historic peoples, the Romans, the Vikings, Anglo-Saxons and Normans have all left evidence of their presence, but have they left ghosts reputed to have been murdered?

Barnard Castle

The 13th century castle was built by Bernard de Balliol overlooking the Tees gorge. The ghost of Lady Ann Day has been seen reliving her ghastly end. She was supposedly pursued across the castle's ramparts, caught and hurled from a tower into the River Tees by her murderer. The reasons why are lost in time.

Some phantoms appear to have died in unusual circumstances.

Barnard Castle consists of a circular tower, a 3-storey keep and a 14th century great hall.

Beamish Hall, Beamish Burn

The hall was built as a wedding gift for Guiscard de Charron in 1268 and has had many occupants including the Percy and Shafto families.

Its most famous ghost is the Grey Lady who announces her presence by the rustling of her wedding dress. One report is of a vet who decided to raise money for charity by sleeping in the hall overnight. Next day he told of seeing the ghost of this woman. Apparently she was forced into an arranged marriage and to avoid it hid in a trunk, but suffocated.

Occasionally a building, which was originally a church, is reputed to be the scene of supernatural phenomena.

Four Clock's Tower, Bishop Auckland

The tower is a former church where there have been many strange occurrences. The sound of footsteps in an empty room has been heard and doors mysteriously locked, but from the inside. In early 2009 the apparition of a woman wearing a hat was seen and CCTV appeared to record a ghostly figure.

Left: The Wesleyan Methodist Church on Newgate Street, Bishop Auckland, in the 1930s. The former church is now known as the Four Clocks Centre.

Another woman is the focus of the next tale.

Lumley's Wronged Woman
August 1631

Ann Walker looked after, her kinsman John Walker's house, at Lumley, near Chester-le Street. He was a widower with a *'good estate'*. Anne was supposedly pregnant, but refused to reveal who the father was. She was sent to her aunt's who lived in the same town. Mark Sharp, from Lancashire, *'a sworn brother'* to John Walker, called Anne from her aunt's home. Anne was never seen again.

Fourteen days later, a fuller called Graham or Graime, who lived at a mill six miles away reported to a JP that he had repeatedly seen the apparition of a woman who made threats and had five wounds to her head. He stated that she said she was *'the spirit of Anne Walker'* who had been murdered and told him where the deed had taken place.

A search was made and Anne's body was discovered in a coal pit. She had five wounds to her head. Sharp's bloody stockings and shoes were found with her. Sharp and Walker were apprehended, but bailed to the next assizes where they were found guilty of murder and executed. (*Sykes, Vol. II, Addenda, p.369.*)

An apparition has been seen at Washington Old Hall.

Washington Old Hall

The 17th century hall incorporates part of the medieval manor house belonging to the direct ancestors of George Washington, the first President of the United States of America. The hall supposedly entertains the ghost of a woman wearing a long dress who haunts the upper floors.

Left: Washington Old Hall – When William de Hertburn became owner of the manor of Washington in 1153, he adopted the name of his new estate and became William de Wessyngton, from which the surname Washington is derived.

Ghosts are one thing, finding ancient objects or treasure is quite another.

Finds and Treasure Hoards
Stone Chests
October, 1716

A mason digging at Glanton Westfield, near Deer Street discovered four chests. One was empty, but the others each contained two urns. Inside were bones bearing marks of a fire, charcoal and earth. On being exposed to the air, the urns cracked. Were these early cremations?

The next find near Alnwick tells us more about the lives of earlier people.

Tools of War and Trade
1726

About a mile north-west of Alnwick, a mason uncovered the earth from a rock in Hulne Park. He found sixteen spear heads and twenty brass swords near the surface. Further down the hill there were cuts in a rock and 42 broken and battered brass wedges or chisels. Who owned them?

The masons' finds are of historical interest, but the following discoveries should strike a chord. Most of us have gone to sleep reading stories about discovering buried treasure. Here are several tales about those who found it. The first took place in Corbridge.

Roman Silver
February, 1735

A smith's daughter found a piece of antique silver when she strolled by a brook to the east of Corbridge, near Hadrian's Wall. Shaped like a 'tea-board', it was 15 inches wide and 20 inches long. It had a brim and was decorated with a vine laden with grapes, Apollo holding a bow, Minerva with a helmet and spear and a priestess. On the back, possibly scratched by a chisel or punch, was an unintelligible inscription.

Mr Cookson, a Newcastle goldsmith must have thought it was a bargain when he bought it for £40, but the Duke of Somerset, being lord of the manor of Corbridge, claimed it. He got an injunction to prevent the goldsmith from defacing, melting it down or selling it. Cookson must have felt disgruntled when his friends persuaded him to hand over the silver to the duke and wait for his decision on the matter. However, the duke ordered that the goldsmith be given more than he paid for the item. The silver later came into the possession of the Duke of Northumberland, who married the heiress and granddaughter of the Duke of Somerset, but who was the original owner?

It is hard luck if the finder suddenly discovers he has no right to the hoard.

Hadrian's Wall at Housesteads. Begun in AD 136, it took 14 years to complete.

The Neville's Cross Hoard
January 30th, 1756

Little did Mr George Smith from Burn Hall know when he hired a labourer to work on his hedge, that he would find a pot of silver coins dating from the time of Edward III of England, Robert II and David of Scotland.

The coins were taken to a Durham silversmith, but the dean and chapter claimed them as treasure trove, stating they were found in the manor of Elvet. The dean divided the money by giving ten coins to himself; five each to his prebendaries (senior members of the clergy) and some were placed in the library. Those that were defaced were sold. The coins were worth £4 to £5.

The Battle of Neville's Cross took place near the site of this find in 1346 and it is likely the coins were deposited here at this time.

Most children dream about finding treasure. The ones in the following account did.

Quids In
June 11th, 1815

A number of children were playing in a brick yard near Shieldfield in Newcastle. They found several guineas in rubbish which had been deposited there from the Grey Horse public house. The news spread and many of those who searched the site also found coins.

The cartman responsible for the rubbish remembered he had dumped another lot from the same pub at a brick yard near Bridge Street, he found seven guineas. One man went at night with a lantern and found a stash of gold and a girl discovered 22 guineas. Most coins were dated 1777, but some were from 1759.

It is thought the coins may have been stolen from a traveller robbed in the Grey Horse about forty years before. Suspicion had fallen on a servant who was sacked and perhaps did not have the opportunity to dig up his or her ill gotten gains.

The landlord of the Grey Horse is reported to have said on his death bed that he had a substantial amount of money, but nothing was found.

Two treasure hoards have been discovered on an island off the North East coast.

The Lindisfarne Hoards

When Henry VIII dissolved the monasteries, stones from Lindisfarne Priory were used to build a small castle and fortify the harbour. Lindisfarne became an armed camp. The first hoard was found in 1962, in a stoneware jug in a house within the old garrison. The hoard consisted of fifty silver 16th century English and Scottish coins which are now housed in the Great North Museum.

Unbelievably the second hoard was found in a similar jug in the same building, but in 2002 by Rothbury builder Robert Mason. He had left the jug in his garage till he finally decided to clean it in 2011. He found ten gold coins and seven silver coins dating from 1430-1562. The English coins span the reigns of six English sovereigns.

The foreign coins include a silver thaler from the Electorate of Saxony, two gold ecus from Francis I of France and a rare gold scudo from Pope Clement VII. In 1562 the hoard would have been worth what £30,000 is today. It is thought the original owner may have been a military officer who had served in England as well as abroad.

Lindisfarne Priory. King Oswald (634-42), a Northumbrian king, granted the monk Aidan, Lindisfarne on which to found a monastery.

Section Three – Mayhem

Most people wish to live in a peaceful world. They want to have families and prosper. In the past for many this was impossible, though they may have experienced some halcyon periods of stability.

Invasions

The following is an example of the Scottish and English working together, well ... to some extent.

Scottish Spoils
1098

Edgar, heir to the throne of Scotland, sent Carileph, Bishop of Durham a token of friendship. Flambard, Carileph's successor, ignored this invaded Scotland and took his spoils back to Durham. Edgar infuriated by this, '*act of hostility and ingratitude complained to William Rufus, King of England ...*' who ordered immediate restitution and gave Berwick to the see of Durham. (*Sykes, Vol. I, p.17.*)

Peace between England and Scotland must have seemed a rarity. Here are several accounts about Scottish raids into Durham and Northumberland.

Scots invade England
1135

'*David, King of Scots, entered England and took Alnwick Castle and other chief places near the northern frontier ...*' In 1138 he also, '*besieged Norham Castle; a gallant defence was made for some time, but the castle being thinly garrisoned, and no succours arriving, the place was surrendered and the troops permitted to retire to Durham. The Scots, on this occasion, destroyed the town and castle. That part of the Scottish army that plundered the western parts of Northumberland, while David ravaged its shores, were encamped at Warden, near Hexham.*'
(*Sykes, Vol. I, p. 18.*)

Right: Norham Castle defended a key ford over the River Tweed. It was besieged at least 13 times and Robert the Bruce laid siege to it for almost a year. It fell in 1513 to James IV just before his Flodden defeat.

Berwick-on-Tweed, because of its strategic position on the eastern coast of the River Tweed just over two miles from the Scottish border, was fought over by the Scots and English and changed hands several times.

A Town in Turmoil
1173-74

Berwick and the surrounding countryside were in ashes and the following year Earl Duncan butchered the town's inhabitants. (*Sykes, Vol. I, p. 21.*)

The Scots did not stop at Berwick, but often continued south.

A Land Laid Waste
1174

England was invaded by William, King of Scotland. He laid waste along the banks of the Tyne and besieged both Prudhoe and Alnwick Castle. William was captured by Ralph de Glanville and four hundred knights and taken to Newcastle. Henry II ordered William to be held

Since the 14th century Alnwick Castle has been home to the Percy family, the Dukes of Northumberland.

in Richmond Castle, then Rouen, Normandy. He was later ransomed at York for £4,000. The people of Newcastle had fought in numerous encounters against this Scottish king so it was inevitable that a ' ... *dreadful encounter took place at the bridge ...*' This was the last time a Scottish king attempted to retrieve land in this area. *(Sykes, Vol. I, p. 21.)*

In the late 13th century the Scots rebelled.

Berwick Again
March 24th, 1295

King Edward I of England, known as Longshanks, was not someone with whom you could disagree. When Baliol, King of Scotland, rebelled, Edward took Berwick by force, but not before the townspeople burnt three of his ships.

The castle was taken and the garrison consisting of two hundred men had to promise they would never bear arms against England again, before they were allowed to march out. Some sources state 7,000 of the inhabitants perished. Thirty Flemings held out for a day in Red Hall, but when it was set on fire they died in the flames. The streets were said to run red with blood like a mill stream for two days.

Edward I complained to Pope Boniface that '*The Scots inhumanely destroyed an innumerable multitude of his subjects, burnt monasteries, churches and towns with an unpitying cruelty ...*' He went on to write that Scottish army had cut off women's breasts, slain women giving birth and babies. They had also locked two hundred young men in a school and burnt it to the ground.
(Sykes, Vol.1, page 32.)

One of four gates in Berwick's town walls built in 1558 in defence against the Scots. An earlier wall was built by Edward I and was two miles long.

The coat of arms of George I over the main gate of Ravensdowne Barracks (1671-1736), Berwick.

William Wallace came to the fore at this point. He was a Scottish knight, landowner and an educated man. The Scots regarded him as a martyr, the English as a traitor, outlaw and murderer responsible for horrendous acts of cruelty.

William Wallace
1297

Northumberland was a dangerous place in which to live. When news came that William Wallace and his Scots were on the way, many Northumbrians fled to Newcastle.

Wallace set fire to Hexham, the school house, the priory and the west end of the church. Corbridge was destroyed and the Benedictine nuns at Lambley were raped and tortured.

The inhabitants of Ryton, thinking they were well defended and that Wallace's marauders would not cross the Tyne, spoke in such strong terms to the Scottish army that the invaders forded the river and plundered the town.

Newcastle townsmen fought off the Scots and there was battle near Alnwick, but Wallace left a trail of destruction as he retreated. He took Berwick, though not the castle and burnt Carham Abbey.

Wallace was later betrayed to the English, taken to London and hanged, drawn and quartered on August 23rd, 1305. The English invented this punishment for him. Half of his body was displayed on Berwick Bridge. His brother Neil and others of note captured with him were taken to Berwick and executed in the same way.

The Wallace monument stands on the summit of Abbey Craig. Completed in 1869, it was designed by John Thomas Rochead and cost £18,000.

In the 14th century Robert the Bruce, King of Scotland invaded Northumberland and County Durham.

Robert the Bruce
1312

Hexham and Corbridge were burnt and Hartlepool was pillaged. Despite the Scottish army trying to take Berwick by surprise, a barking dog roused the inhabitants and saved them.

When Robert the Bruce defeated Edward II at the Battle of Bannockburn in 1314 the English borders became an even more dangerous place to live. The Scottish army were '*laying Northumberland and Durham under heavy contribution ... In the succeeding year they again penetrated into the bishopric, where they ... plundered Hartlepool.*' (Sykes, Vol. I, p. 34.)

Left: The Robert the Bruce monument at Bannockburn, Stirling.

Both Wallace and Bruce attacked Hexham and Corbridge.

Hexham Abbey founded in AD 674. It was formerly an Augustinian priory church of St Andrew and a Benedictine monastery.

Vicar's Pele is a pele tower in Corbridge. Built about AD 1300 for a Corbridge vicar, it was inhabited until the early 17th century.

On a lighter note …

Sounds Painful!
1316

The Scottish army invaded as far as Durham *'and burnt the prior's seat at Beaurpaire.'*

Most men fought for their country and few were traitors. Hailed as a hero by the Americans and French during the War of American Independence (1775-83) and in modern times, John Paul Jones has been called many things by the British, notorious and pirate were probably amongst the more repeatable. Why?

John Paul Jones
September 23rd, 1779

He was born John Paul in Kirkcudbright, Scotland on July 6th, 1747. The son of a gardener, he went to sea at 13 years of age and served aboard a merchant ship 'Friendship' operating out of Whitehaven.

In his early sailing years, whilst learning his trade, he sailed on trading ships and slavers. Sickened by the latter trade, he sailed from the West Indies as the mate on the 'John' in 1768. When the captain died of yellow fever, John Paul took command and sailed the ship back to Whitehaven. The owners made him the permanent captain at twenty-one years of age.

John Paul Jones.

Whitehaven harbour entrance.

Within two years his reputation was in tatters for having flogged a sailor who died two weeks later. Whilst off Tobago in 1773 as captain of the, 'Betsy' he had problems with his crew and was forced to shoot one of them in self defence. He fled knowing the admiralty commission meant to hear his case and put him on trial. When his brother died, John Paul changed his name to John Paul Jones.

Whitehaven Harbour.

During the War of American Independence Jones became a captain in the Continental Navy. His reputation increased whilst sailing on the 'Providence' as he captured numerous British vessels.

On April 11th, 1778 he sailed into the Irish Sea hoping to take the war to the British. Jones had a working knowledge of Whitehaven. It was Britain's busiest port with fortifications, guns and a harbour full of 400 British merchant ships.

Whitehaven's fortifications.

There are many versions of what happened next, this is mine. On April 22nd, 1778 Commander John Paul Jones anchored 'USS Ranger' two miles off Whitehaven. His plan was to arrive at midnight, the time when the ebb tide would leave ships at their most vulnerable. He and thirty volunteers, armed with pistols and cutlasses, and in two boats rowed into Whitehaven harbour. It was hard going and they did not arrive until dawn.

Jones and twenty men landed at the end of the Old Quay at the battlements. They took the southern battery and spiked the cannon. The second boat, consisting of ten disgruntled men led by Lieutenant of Marines Samuel Willingsford/Wallingford, disgorged at the Old Quay slip. The men had expected to capture ships, not sink them. Unhappy they would not receive a share of the profits, they entered a public house Nich Allison's on the Old Quay and drank their alcohol whilst holding the family prisoner.

Above: The watchtower and Nich Allison's public house on the Old Quay.

Left: Close up Nich Allison's pub and stone steps on the Old Quay.

The 'Thompson' laden with coal, and lying close to a staithe, was boarded. Two boys were taken off and the vessel set alight. The idea was that its falling mast would set the next ship on fire and so on. The boys were offered money to join Jones' men which they refused. Dressed only in shirts and with a handkerchief gag in their mouths, the boys were held under guard on the quay. They were told not to shout a warning or they would be shot.

One report states that the second boat was unsuccessful in attacking the northern battery. Another account says that most of the guns at both forts had been spiked and on board vessels were several matches which were made of canvas and dipped in brimstone. Yet another report states that Jones set fire to

Statue depicting spiking the guns.

the southern battery and flames spread to the whole of Whitehaven.

Two newspapers 'Lloyd's Evening Post' and 'The Cumberland Chronicle' record that one of Jones' men, David Freeman, possibly an Irishman, managed to slip away. Perhaps his conscience got the better of him. He ran to Marlborough Street, just off the quay, and rapped on doors to warn the inhabitants that the 'Thompson' was aflame, other ships soon would be and Whitehaven was about to be destroyed.

Fortunately, the fire on the 'Thompson' was extinguished, and the matches thrown onto ships went out. Depending on which side of the Atlantic you are, the raid or invasion may be regarded as bold or bungled. It certainly had the effect of sending British ports into a panic and Jones himself said, ' ... *what was done ... is sufficient to show that not all their boasted navy can protect their coasts ...*'

Jones went on to sail round Scotland and attempted to kidnap Lord Selkirk to exchange him for American prisoners of war. Selkirk was not at home so Jones took his silver plate instead. One item was a silver teapot full of breakfast tea. Jones then appeared off the coast of Northumberland for a day and captured a sloop. This caused uproar in the North East. The Duke of Northumberland's bailiff was convinced Jones was after the duke's rents, mostly gold, lying in Alnwick Castle. One can only imagine the panic when the commander of the Huntingdon militia was called to garrison the castle and prepare its defences. The gates were barricaded and cannons put at the ready. Jones ignored the castle and sailed on.

He met the Baltic fleet near Flamborough Head, Yorkshire and took part in a sea battle. Jones flotilla comprised of the 'Vengeance' an armed brig containing 12 guns and 70 men; 'The Pallas' a French frigate carrying 30 guns and 275 men; the 'Alliance' a frigate of 40 guns and 300 men and his own ship 'USS Bonhomme Richard' an American ship of war of 40 guns and 375 men.

When 'USS Bonhomme Richard' was hit and started taking on water, Jones was ordered to surrender by the captain of the British ship 'Serapis'. Jones replied, '*I have not yet begun to fight.*' Hours later he was the victor when he defeated the 'Serapis'. Jones was victorious having completely outgunned the British. He captured two ships, 'Serapis', a frigate with 44 guns, and an armed ship of 20 guns, 'Countess of Scarborough'.

I suspect seaman 'Old Taylor of Cullercoats' called Jones some choice names having lost an arm and an eye in this naval engagement. Taylor's portrait was painted and lithographed by Mr Parker from Newcastle.

In America Jones is regarded as one of the most successful and daring commanders of the American Revolution and father of the American navy. He died aged 45 in 1792 and was buried in a cemetery on the outskirts of Paris. In 1905 he was reburied in a crypt in Annapolis, Maryland, USA. On the marble floor in front of his sarcophagus are the following words:

'JOHN PAUL JONES. 1747-1792; U.S. NAVY 1775-1783 HE GAVE OUR NAVY ITS TRADITIONS OF HEROISM AND VICTORY. ERECTED BY CONGRESS, A.D. 1912.'

Treason

The Glorious Revolution of 1689 meant Roman Catholic James II fled the country and Protestant William of Orange and his wife Mary (James II's daughter) were invited to rule instead.

This was a great disappointment to those who wanted Roman Catholicism as the main religion in Great Britain and a relief for those who believed that papists were openly plotting to overturn a Protestant government. This fear and yearning for the return of the Stuart dynasty would rumble on over two centuries.

Sir John Fenwick
January 27th, 1697

Sir John Fenwick, of Wallington, Northumberland was an MP and apparently well thought of, being described as, ' ... *a man of considerable talent* ...' and having, '... *splendid traits in his character.*'

Unfortunately, in 1694 he assisted in plans to restore James II to the throne and overthrow King William III. Realising the government knew about the plot, he attempted to escape to France in 1696, but was captured at New Romney, Kent, '*committed to the tower and indicted at the Old Bailey for compassing and imagining the death and destruction of the king, and adhering to his enemies.*' A law was, ' ... *made on purpose to stain the scaffold with his blood* ...' He was not hanged, drawn and quartered as the law allowed, but beheaded on Tower Hill, London. It is thought the high rank of Lady

Wallington Hall is an early 17th century mansion built around a pele tower and medieval house.

These griffin heads came from Old Aldersgate in London and were brought in ballast to the North East in one of Sir William Blackett's ships.

Fenwick being Lady Mary Howard, eldest daughter of Charles, Earl of Carlisle, meant his estates were not forfeited.

Fenwick at 52 years of age showed, *'great firmness and composure'* when meeting his fate. He was buried near his three sons by the altar of St Martin's Church, London. *' ... good men pitied his death on account of the harsh and unconstitutional measures by which it was accomplished.' (Sykes, Vol. I, p. 126.)*

Ordinary men can also commit extraordinary acts. With a forename like Lancelot, I suppose we should not be surprised that Lancelot Errington like so many others was involved in the 1715 Jacobite rebellion. Unfortunately he was on the side which lost. The following tale is one of daring, bravery and adventure.

A Tale of Derring-Do

The '15'

Lancelot Errington, from Northumberland was the master of a ship and a follower of the Stuart cause. He had been promised help from several French privateers and Mr Forster the rebel's general, if he took the castle on Lindisfarne.

The castle's garrison consisted of about twelve men under a corporal and sergeant. Errington invited the sergeant and his men aboard his ship where they were plied with brandy until they were drunk.

Errington returned to the castle with his nephew, Mark Errington. They knocked the sentry to the ground whilst a corporal, two other soldiers and an old gunner were thrown out of the castle and the Pretender's flag raised. The promised reinforcements did not arrive, but the king's troop from Berwick did.

Escaping over the castle walls, the Erringtons hoped to conceal themselves amongst the rocks and seaweed until night fell and they could swim to the mainland.

Unfortunately the tide rose, Lancelot was wounded in the thigh and the men were forced to surrender. They were taken to Berwick Gaol until Lancelot's wound healed. However, they dug their way out and escaped with other prisoners, most of whom were recaptured.

Making their way to the Tweed, the Erringtons stole a custom-house boat, rowed across the river and turned the boat adrift. They went to Bamburgh Castle where a relative provided them with provisions whilst they

The 16th century Lindisfarne Castle. (Courtesy of E. and N. Windham.)

Lindisfarne Causeway. (Courtesy of E. and N. Windham.)

Lindisfarne. (Courtesy of E. and N. Windham.)

hid for nine days in a pea stack. Leaving their hideout, they made their way to Gateshead and obtained passage from Sunderland to France. A reward of £500 was offered for their capture, despite this Lancelot visited friends in Newcastle.

The Erringtons remained free and took advantage of the general pardon after the rebellion. They returned to Newcastle and Lancelot died there in 1746, some say of grief, when he heard of the Hanoverian victory at Culloden. Lancelot and his nephew were fortunate, but thirty years later Thomas Collingwood was not quite so lucky.

Collingwood's Capers
1745

'*Northumberland – Whereas Thomas Collingwood, of Thrunton, in this county, was committed on Wednesday last to the gaol, in and for this county, at Morpeth, for high treason, and made his escape from thence, in the night between the 27th and 28th of this instant, November; These are therefore to give notice, that if any person, or persons shall apprehend the said Thomas Collingwood, and deliver him to the keeper of the said gaol, such person or persons shall have paid to him or them, by the treasurer of this county, a reward of £50. N.B. The said Thomas Collingwood is a person of middle stature, about 25 years of age, has a round face, and a short nose, and wore, when he escaped, a light coloured wig, a dark coloured coat, and a silk handkerchief about his neck.*'
(*Sykes, Vol.1, p.177.*)

Collingwoood was captured, taken to Carlisle, tried with other prisoners from the '45 rebellion and acquitted on September 19th, 1746. The majority of captured rebels were either hanged or transported.

Mobs and Riots

'*Whatever the cause of riots might be, the real one is always want of happiness. It shows that something is wrong with the system of government.*' Thomas Paine

From Pride to Fall
October 2nd 1648

Thomas Bonner, Esq must have been pleased with himself as he had just become the elected Mayor of Newcastle. As night fell, Bonner's way was lit by torches carried by sergeants as he triumphantly journeyed from the Spittle to his home on Sandhill. Unfortunately, Edmund Marshall spoilt the day by hurling a large stick at the torches. Darkness descended, several stones were hurled and the stately procession was thrown into disarray as the mayor and his followers raced to safety.

Right: Sandhill, Newcastle, is where wealthy merchants used to live in the 16-17th century houses.

The rise of the mob was always of concern to the authorities. When corn was scarce and therefore too expensive to buy, the militia were called in to deal with the starving lower classes.

Corn Riot
March 27th, 1801

Dealers were demanding forty shillings for a boll (140lbs) of wheat in Sunderland's corn market. The starving populace could not contain their anger and they smeared a farmer with dirt from the kennels. He fled to the safety of the Fountain Inn, but the crowd attacked it, the Half Moon and the Queen's Head with stones and brick-bats. The houses on either side were also damaged in the affray. The mob trampled corn under their feet and a number of farmers' carts ended up in the River Wear. One was even seen floating out at sea the following day.

A JP and constables arrested one man and held him in the Cape, but the rioters helped him escape. At 9 pm when more constables arrived and candles were lit, the Riot Act was read on the steps of the George Inn. It made little difference and the JP ensured the military guarded his house throughout the night. The Lancashire militia were also called out and though muskets were loaded, they were not ordered to fire.

There was also a riot over forged coins.

The Sunderland Mob
September 18th, 1816

Was someone trying to pass forged coins in Sunderland? Several shopkeepers were suspicious of the plain shillings and sixpences being offered and refused to accept them. Not to be thwarted, later that night, a mob descended on the shops of 'Andrews', 'Messrs Caleb Wilson', 'Nattrass Middlebrook', 'Hall' and 'Walton' and broke their windows. The shops all sold either groceries or flour. Rioters swarmed into Middlebrook's premises and were seen running out carrying hams, bacon and groceries.

At midnight the 33rd regiment were called out and the Riot Act was read. The mob took bricks stacked at a house being rebuilt for a surgeon, Mr Barnes, and threw them at the soldiers causing injuries amongst their ranks. It was only then the rioters dispersed.

Innovations could mean unemployment and destitution for workers and their families.

Rioting Keelmen
March 20th, 1820

Keelmen (worked on boats which carried coal from shore to collier ships) and casters (loaded coal onto ships) working on the River Wear in Sunderland were incensed. Not only had a bridge been built at Galley's Gill near Bishopwearmouth, for conveying 'Messrs. Nesham and Co's' coal wagons to the staithes below, but there were rumours that more staithes were about to be built. This meant keelmen and casters would no longer be required and would become unemployed.

A riotous group set the staithes alight at the head of the bridge as well as the machinery which took the wagons down to the spouts where coal was deposited onto ships. They then pulled

The Sunderland staithes at Galley's Gill.

down a house and took several rooves off others destroying property worth about £6,000 in the process.

The riot only stopped when late into the night a *'party of horse arrived from Newcastle and dispersed the mob.'* One man was killed by falling timbers. (*Sykes, Vol. II, page 89.*)

A group of keelmen on the quayside.

Keelmen were renowned for being prepared to fight for their rights as were colliers. In 1831 wastemen used the waste from the colliery to build supporting pillars and ensure ventilation of the mine. They worked under the direction of the viewer who was responsible for handling waste products and mine ventilation. Goodness knows what wasteman William Garth said or did that incensed his workmates so much they decided to teach him a lesson.

Five Or More Against One
1831

It was May 17th and William Garth worked at Mount Moor Colliery. He was walking home from work to get his dinner when he was confronted by an angry mob. Thirty year old John Routledge seized Garth and threw him into a pond which was 5-6 feet deep. Some of the mob waded into the water, stood on him and tried to prevent him breathing. When he eventually got to the bank they covered his face in cow dung, stripped him and threw him in the pond again. When Garth made it back to dry land he realised his sleeve was being held by twenty-seven year old John Storey.

In court, Garth recognised John Routledge, Ralph Wakefield (28), John Storey (27), Ralph Cooper (37) and William Richardson (23). He stated that he did not see Cooper, Wakefield or Richardson do anything to him.

When Garth was cross-examined he admitted he had told several people he *' ... could not swear to any of the men because he was afraid for his life.'* However, Mr. Seymour, the viewer at Mount Moor Colliery said he had seen all the prisoners amongst the mob. Storey and Routledge were found guilty and sentenced to two years hard labour. The other men were acquitted. (*The Newcastle Courant, July 29th, 1831*).

Law and order and alcohol do not always go hand in hand.

Pub Fights

The text below is originally from an 18th century poster that was discovered by one of the demolition team behind a picture in The Mitre public house in Stanhope Road, Newcastle. It lists rules that had to be displayed in Newcastle's 18th century public houses and gives us a good idea of what went on inside them.

Newcastle, April 30th, 1788

RULES to be observed by all Persons who shall here-after be Licensed to keep Common Ale or Victualling Houses, in this Town and County, upon Pain of Forfeiting their respective Licenses.

1st That no Publican shall suffer any Guests or Company to be in his or her House, Yard &c drinking or idleing during the time of Divine Service on Sundays, either in the Forenoon or Afternoon, nor later any Night throughout the Year than Ten o'Clock, but that every Publican shall keep his or her House, and Doors, shut up at those Times against all his Guests, except Travellers.

2d That no Publican shall suffer any Apprentices, Servants, Journey-men Pitmen, Keelmen, Labourers, or other Persons in poor or low Stations of Life, to waste their Time and Money by tipling longer, or drinking more in his or her House or Yard, &c. than shall be necessary for their Refreshment and moderate comfort.

3d That no Publican shall harbour, lodge, or entertain any Felons, Thieves, Rogues, Vagrants, Smugglers, Sharpers, Swindlers, lewd Women or any Persons of ill Fame, nor suffer any such to resort to his or her House, nor conceal, buy, or receive any stolen or smuggled Goods.

4d That no Publican shall suffer any Manner of Gaming, Sharping, Swindling, or Fraud, or any Quarrelling, Fighting, Brawling, Cursing, Swearing, Drunkenness, Lewdness, unlawful Associations and Conspiracies or any other Disorder, in his or

Hell's Kitchen at the Flying Horse – a notorious Newcastle pub.

her House, or Yard &c. but as often as any of the aforesaid Disorders begin, shall his or her utmost endeavours to prevent the same, by sending for one of the of the nearest or first Serjeants at Mace, Constables, or Peace Officers, than can be had; and by calling in other Assistance, to take the Offenders before a Magistrate, and all other Persons are required to assist the Serjeants at Mace, Constables, and Peace Officers therein.

5th That no Publican shall refuse to open his or her Doors to any Church Wardens, Chapel Wardens, Serjeants at Mace, Constables or Peace Officers, at any Time, when they are upon their Duty, nor shall hinder them from entering his or her House, or from doing their Duty therein.

6th The Mayor and Magistrates have resolved, that at the next general Licencing of Common Alehouse-keepers, and Victuallers in this Town, a printed Copy of these Rules and also his Majesty's Proclamation, for preventing and punishing Vice, Profaneness, and Immorality, shall be delivered with every Licence to or for every Person Licenced, Therefore every such Licenced Person shall keep the said two printed Copies constantly hanging up, either in frames or pasted on Boards, in the most proper and conspicuous

place in his or her House, where all Persons resorting to the House, may read the same; and every Publican who shall wilfully disobey, or knowingly transgress any of the aforesaid Rules, he or she so offending, shall (besides being deprived of his or her Licence) be further prosecuted as the Law directs.
By order. CLAYTON

The poster makes it obvious what had taken place and what those in charge of law and order in Newcastle in 1778 and his 'Majesty' found unacceptable: *'Vice, Profananeness, and Immorality'.* The onus was placed upon the poor publican not to break these rules.

I suspect many of us would now like to sit in an old Newcastle public house and watch the characters and goings on with mounting interest. At least we can read about some of them.

Shades of Stranger Danger
February 13th, 1833

Guiseppe Sidoli probably went in the Shades public house, Gordon Chare, Newcastle to have a quiet pint. In Italy it may have been acceptable to sit down and join a group of strangers who were drinking, apparently it was not in the Shades.

There was a scuffle and Sidoli was outnumbered. Concerned for his own safety, Sidoli stabbed Irishman, Hugh Ross in the abdomen. Ross was rushed to the Infirmary, but died several days later.

On February 23rd, Sidoli was tried at the Assizes and found guilty of manslaughter.

He was sentenced to seven years transportation.

Most people if they were suspected of murder would keep a low profile.

Innocent or Guilty?
September, 1840

Thomas Burn, whilst sitting in a public house in Sunderland, invited the victim's brother, Cadell, to drink with him. Cadell replied, *'What, drink with my brother's murderer?'* Burn threw his drink in Cadell's face and tried to escape. Cadell found a policeman, Burn was arrested and taken to the town where the murder had taken place. *(Fordyce & Sykes, Vol. III, p.136-137.)*

A Sunderland pub in the mid 19th century – the Three Crowns Hotel with wagon in front.

The following riot took place because of alcohol and a series of misunderstandings.

'The Green Tree' Riot
June 7th, 1841

Mrs M'Gallon was the 'hostess' of the Green Tree public house in Sandgate, Newcastle. In the early afternoon a number of public houses in Sandgate were filled with soldiers and she was probably pleased when several men from the 87th regiment, stationed at the barracks, came to the Green Tree and ordered drinks, after all, this would not have harmed her takings.

However, the drunken behaviour of three soldiers gave her and her neighbours such cause for concern that she decided to call the police who lifted one semi-conscious soldier from the floor and set him on his way back to the barracks. Unfortunately, someone was overheard saying he was being taken to the station house. Thinking he was being arrested, five soldiers rushed to rescue him. The police stood their ground which resulted in a couple of them being knocked down by fists and canes as others defended themselves with batons.

The populace joined in with the soldiers against the police. A riot had begun! At one point over 5,000 people were gathered and it was only with great difficulty that the fighting ceased. The regiment, undoubtedly in disgrace, was ordered to Hull.

Old inns, the Bigg Market, Newcastle in the 1840s.

Being the landlady of a public house proved too much for some.

A Desperate Act at the Duke of Cumberland Arms
July 10th, 1842

Why would someone throw themselves out of an attic window? Mrs Isabella Carnaby, landlady of the Duke of Cumberland Arms, did. She landed on the street below and died shortly afterwards.

As we saw in the riot at the Green Tree soldiers can be difficult to handle.

The Soldiers' Lot

Mutiny
September 9th, 1795

The 23rd or Ulster regiment of light dragoons arrived in Newcastle on the 9th and did not want to be disbanded. There were numerous meetings where the privates let it be known in no uncertain manner that they did not want to be parted from their friends and drafted into other regiments. Despite this, they felt their pleas were being ignored when they heard a rumour that the regiment was going to be incorporated into the 21st, Lord Beaumont's light dragoons.

That evening the soldiers of the 23rd gathered in angry groups all over Newcastle. At 5 pm a party broke into the repository for the regimental stores and snatched a large supply of gunpowder and balls.

The 4th regiment of dragoons were summoned to Newcastle at 9 pm followed by the 37th regiment of foot at 11 pm. Some of the soldiers guarded the town gates; others patrolled the streets and the rest were given the dangerous job of taking the weapons and ammunition from the mutinous troops.

Next morning the 23rd were paraded in Northumberland Street. General Smith explained why the disbanding of their regiment was necessary. The soldiers then complained that they had not been paid a bounty they had been promised. The general assured them they would be paid the arrears before noon the following day.

A small handbill was distributed after this mutiny:

A CAUTION to the Inhabitants of Newcastle upon Tyne
As there is a reason to suppose that some ill disposed-people in town are endeavouring to foment disturbances amongst the military, This earnestly a request, That all sober-minded inhabitants will refrain from collecting in the Streets, lest from idle Curiosity, they should mix with these ill-intentioned people, and expose themselves to the Misfortunes that may happen.
Mansion-house, 9th September, 1795
(Sykes, Vol.1, p.376.)

Most of us would fight to the death for our families, but would we do the same for a goat?

A Fight over a Goat!
November 25th, 1796

The army at this time was usually involved in fighting battles or quelling rioting peasants. It is hard to understand why soldiers would be prepared to kill each other over a goat.

The Westminster militia and Lowland Scot fencibles were quartered in Sunderland. The fencibles had a tame regimental goat which was *'wantonly killed'* by a member of the militia. The goat had been very popular with the fencibles and they took the matter very seriously indeed. So much so they drew up in battle order *'under arms'* and *'sent a defiance'* (a challenge) to the militia. This was accepted.

The militia joined the fencibles on the barrack ground and a bloody outcome was expected until Prince William of Gloucester, *'after firm and strenuous exertions'* intervened and peace was restored. The main instigators were tried by court martial. *(Sykes, Vol. 1, p. 382.)*

Some regiments have ponies as mascots.

There seems to be a pattern of behaviour amongst the soldiering fraternity.

Just Passing Through
September 19th, 1797

The West Lowland fencibles were quartered in Newcastle and the Cheshire militia were passing through Blyth Camp on their way to Carlisle. Well, that is what should have happened.

Unfortunately there appears to have been no love lost between the two regiments and a fight started. It was night. Presumably, in the darkness the sound of soldiers marching through the streets caused confusion and panic amongst the townsfolk which soon turned to alarm. This is odd as Newcastle is a barrack town and the town's populace should have been used to regiments coming and going. Some of Newcastle's residents became involved in fracas with soldiers involving bayonets and other weapons all over the town. Blood was spilled and many civilians were bruised from the blows they received. It says a lot about Newcastle's fighting civilians that about thirty soldiers were injured, some of them seriously.

The Dumfrieshire light dragoons were called out, stopped the fighting and scoured the streets for any who wished to continue. Next morning on the parade ground General Este, *'acquitted the militia of beginning the riot and promised to bring the offenders to justice if they could be found.'* *(Sykes, Vol. 1, p.385.)*

Fenham Barracks in Newcastle built in 1804-06.

This is a tale about two soldiers who were just trying to get home.

A Bad Weather Tale
February 14th, 1801

Two soldiers from the 3rd Lancashire militia had been given leave. Whilst travelling between Durham and Bishop Auckland in extremely bad weather they found themselves past the point of exhaustion. At some point the soldiers parted company. One spotted a public house near Butcher Row and made straight for a chair by the fire. Whilst warming himself, he fell and died. The other soldier was found dead beside a park wall near Auckland by a butcher going to Durham market.

The next tale is not about bad weather, but of over enthusiastic impressing of men to join the army in Berwick in 1804. A likely recruit would be offered the King's shilling. If it was accepted it meant he was a loyal subject and a candidate for the press. Not unreasonably, many men preferred to stay at home amongst friends and family as conditions on ships and in the military were dreadful if not dangerous, particularly at time of war.

The Press Gang were not averse to bending or breaking rules and would often get a man drunk then plant the King's shilling in his tankard as he had to been seen to take it. A glass bottomed tankard was invented to stop this happening.

Army Recruiters
June 9th, 1804

Perhaps the York Reserve was too enthusiastic in its efforts to persuade the locals to join their ranks in Berwick. Certainly, when one thousand angry male civilians poured onto the street, the soldiers must have been more than a touch concerned as they drew their swords and fixed bayonets.

As the two sides grappled with each other, the air was filled with groans, oaths and blows which would only have increased with the arrival of the main guard who assisted their officers and comrades in arms. Amidst the uproar, the mayor, almost read the Riot Act several times, but he and his officers, magistrates and other gentlemen eventually managed to quell the riot and the soldiers returned to their barracks.

Two men in particular were praised. The chief magistrate was described as manly, spirited and judicious and Captain Locke from the Royal Navy apparently kept a cool head whilst vigorously arguing for peace.

Understandably, many men were extremely reluctant to be recruited into the army or navy. The nature of warfare meant both services continually needed to fill their ranks and this led to conflict when the Impress Service was in town.

Left: The 18th century Ravensdowne Barracks, Berwick-upon-Tweed were designed by Nicholas Hawksmoor.

Tales of the Sea

The 'STAVROS S NIARCHOS' sailing off Blyth in July 2014.

'Three Sisters II' a fishing coble at Newbiggin.

The Press Gang

The Impress Service's origins appear to lie in Elizabethan times with the passing of the Vagrancy Act of 1597 and a statute. Commonly called the Press Gang, their job was to press disreputable men, usually vagrants, into the army or Royal Navy, an even more difficult task at time of war. Volunteers were offered an advance in pay or bounties, but if this failed to provide seamen, then the Impress Service or 'Press' was used.

The 'Press' usually consisted of an officer and twelve men who roamed the countryside, streets, quay sides and public houses looking for recruits. The officer was paid 3d and his men 1d for every mile they travelled. They were also given up to ten shillings for each pressed man delivered to the ship. Merchant seamen were particularly prized as they needed little training.

In 1703 only men under eighteen, except for apprentices could be impressed. The age was raised to 55 in 1744, but the age limits were often ignored. Men could volunteer and receive advance pay for instance, or be impressed and get nothing.

Foreigners had more rights than those who were native born, as they were exempt from being impressed, but could volunteer. However, if a foreigner worked on a British merchant ship for two years or married a British woman, then they forfeited their right not to be impressed, though could still volunteer. Men, if they could afford it, often bribed the 'Press' to get out of their clutches.

North Shields and its skilled seamen were regularly targeted by the Press Gang.

The North East coast, Tyneside and Sunderland were regularly raided by the 'Press'. The area was second only to London in providing seamen and keelmen for the French Wars in the 18th and 19th centuries.

'The Peggy' was one of the naval vessels involved in these raids and is remembered by the area known as 'Peggy's Hole' near North Shields Fish Quay. One poignant ballad, 'Here's the Tender Coming' (a tender transports supplies and or people from another ship to shore) records what it was like:

'Here's the tender comin',
Pressing all the men,
Oh dear hinny, what shall we dee then?
Here's the tender comin';
Off at Shields Bar
Here's the tender comin'
Full of men o' war.
They will ship you foreign,
that is what it means
Here's the tender comin';
Full of Red Marines
So hide me canny Geordie,
Hide yorsel' away,
Wait until the frigate makes for Druridge Bay,
If they tyek yer Geordie,
Wes te' win wor breed?
Me and little Jacky would be better off deed.' (Anon).

During the Napoleonic Wars, Dolly Peel's husband and son were impressed and she would have had to rely on the local parish for support. Dolly was obviously determined that this would not happen to her. She hid aboard their ship and when discovered was told she would have to nurse the wounded and sick. She gained so much respect for what she did for the men that she was allowed to stay on board with her family. Later, pardoned for her initial attempts to interfere with the work of the navy, her husband and son were also exempted from being pressed.

Dolly was from South Shields and quite a character. She is remembered for her stories, wit and as a hawker of contraband goods.

Right: Dolly Peel (1792-1857) statue, River Drive, near junction of Palatine Street, South Shields.

Keelmen were supposed to be exempt from being pressed, but the Press Gang system was open to corruption and they were also pressed. Keelmen's families in Sandgate lived in constant fear in the 18th century because of Captain Bover's Press Gang, which roamed Newcastle quayside. A reminder of Bover is caught in this fragment of a song:

'Aw've been to the Norrard, cruising back and forrard
But danna come ashore for Bover and his men.' (Anon).

A busy scene on Newcastle Quayside.

Once impressed, the men's families did not know what had happened to them. Men could be at sea for years, come back to their home port, set on foot on the quayside and be pressed again. It comes as no surprise that many like William Moffat fought back.

The Barber of ... Swalwell
March 31st, 1759

Moffat, a barber from Swalwell, would probably not have described himself as a swordsman, but when a press gang swooped on him in Newcastle, he drew his sword. A midshipman was badly injured and William Bell received five sword wounds in various parts of his body which eventually killed him.

Bell's widow offered £25 in an advertisement for the barber's apprehension. Moffat was taken at Whitehaven and Mr Osburn received the reward for his capture. Taken to Durham Gaol, Moffat was acquitted in August, 1759.

Desperate men committed desperate deeds. The chances of pressed men escaping were highest when they were first captured as can be seen in the following tales.

Errol Flynn Eat Your Heart Out
May 14th 1759

It was raining heavily. The impressed men lying imprisoned in the hold of a tender moored on the River Wear at Sunderland had no intention of staying where they were. Their leader scrambled up on deck and 'wrested the halberd from the sentry. (A halberd, halbert or Swiss voulge is basically a spear with an axe on the top. It was used for thrusting not throwing.) Using the weapon to defend himself, he let down a ladder with his other hand so his friends could escape from the ship's hold. The impressed men clambered up on deck and knocked down their guards. About thirty men escaped. The capital letter 'R' for Run would have been put against deserters' names.

Some did not just escape; they took the tender on which they were held.

Theft of a Tender
February 12th, 1777

At 8 pm impressed men overpowered the 'Union' tender at Shields and ignoring the fire from Clifford's Fort and other tenders, set out to sea. It was not until February 14th that there was news of their safe arrival in Scarborough.

Often, as can be seen in the next two stories, seamen did everything they could to free the impressed men and the Impress Service responded in the only way they knew how.

Heart of Oakes
February 24th, 1777

Seamen took boats to try to prevent vessels from sailing with impressed men aboard. Lieutenant Oakes and the Impress Service set off after the seamen. He took two blunderbusses loaded with bird shot. Twenty sailors from one boat boarded the 'Present Succession' and gathered on the forecastle with seamen from other ships.

Oakes tried to capture the impressed men whilst sailors rained wood and coal down on top of him and ignored his commands to stop. He threatened them three times with the blunderbuss, but was ignored. When he attempted to fire over their heads, the gun did not go off. Unfortunately, whilst he was examining the weapon, it fired and wounded a sailor on the ship. Oakes and his men were fortunate to escape with their lives. The sailor later died.

Making an Impression
March 13th, 1793

Five hundred sailors were determined to rescue impressed men on board the 'Eleanor'. Armed with pistols and swords they tried to seize the ship, but officers from the Impress Service fought them off.

The following day the seamen attempted to go to Newcastle, but heard that the North York Militia and dragoons had been alerted. At Howden Pass they mistreated one of the Press Gang, George Forster. Their excuse was that the impressed men were being badly treated on the tender.

Some of the population of Newcastle panicked when they thought the sailors were on the way. The dragoons in Newcastle were ordered to hold themselves in readiness, but the sailors did not appear.

Large numbers of men could be impressed at any one time.

Cordon Round North Shields
April 26th, 1793

It was night and at first the people of North Shields must not have known the regiment at Tynemouth barracks had formed a cordon round the town because armed ships in Shields harbour were short of crew. Press Gangs gathered 250 mechanics, sailors, labourers and so on and forced them to board the waiting ships.

COLLINGWOOD MONUMENT TRAFALGAR DAY 1905 —ELLIOTT. PHOTO—

Left: Here is a more heroic view of life in the Navy. The Collingwood Monument at the mouth of the Tyne is decorated for Trafalgar Day.

For local men the urge to escape must have been overpowering as everyone and everything they cared about was ashore.

Attempted Escape
March 9th, 1794

It was about noon and the crew of the tender 'Eleanor' at Shields were eating. The impressed men with the aid of volunteers decided this was the moment to escape. They overcame the sentries, took the ship, but met resistance from the officers and crew. There were wounded on both sides. Some of the impressed men were captured, but many got ashore. Some were taken, others escaped.

Occasionally those who sought to aid the impressed men, were themselves caught and impressed.

Peace Restored?
1796

Shields seamen often *'deprived officers of command and detained vessels underway for sea'*. Seventy to eighty of the seamen's leaders were arrested, impressed and peace on shore restored. *(Sykes, Vol. I, p. 383.)*

Occasionally there were running fights between the victims' friends and family, and the Press Gang. The civil authorities often subverted the process by supporting the pressed men. The Impress Service was not liked, but to some extent was accepted. The Napoleonic Wars of 1803-15 was the last time impressment was used, though the right to impress was retained. It was not untill 1835 that a statute was passed exempting impressed sailors who had served five years in the navy from being impressed again. They were also offered of a pension after having served a set number of years. Being a sailor in the navy was seen to provide long term economic security, even if it could be a dangerous occupation.

Handling explosive materials was also dangerous.

Explosions

A Bright Spark
April 15th, 1757

Mr Green was a shopkeeper from Corbridge. Whilst cleaning his gun, he tested the trigger. A spark fell onto a 10lb box of gunpowder causing an explosion which scorched Green and set his clothes on fire. Four other people were injured in the blast. It was only because a door was open that Green's house was not blown up.

One would have thought soldiers should have known better.

Sergeant Saves the Day
September 15th, 1758

A brave sergeant saved a number of lives and Morpeth's Town Hall through his quick thinking. Apparently a corporal and two sergeants were filling cartridges with gunpowder which was on a table. Somehow the powder ignited and about a thousand cartridges exploded badly burning the three men. One of the sergeants swept two bags of gunpowder and three thousand cartridges off the table and away from the burning cartridges. No one was killed.

Morpeth Town Hall was designed by Sir John Vanbrugh in 1714.

73

The invention of the Humphrey Davy lamp should have reduced the risk of explosions in mines.

Moody's Mad Moment
June 30th, 1817

Apparently John Moody was an obstinate man who worked in Row Pit, Harraton Colliery, on the River Wear. One source certainly blames him for the disaster that follows. Perhaps he thought he always knew best or that he had never had a problem with a lit candle down a pit before or that the worst could never happen to him. Moody was relieving two workmen and defied the overman's orders. He did not use Sir Humphry Davy's safety lamp and lit a candle instead. The workmen doused the flame twice. Moody determinedly relit the candle by unscrewing the lamp. The carburetted hydrogen gas in the pit ignited! Moody, his two companions and 35 other pitmen died in the explosion. The death toll included a grandfather, two sons and seven grandsons from the Hills family.

The St Hilda Colliery Banner – one of a number of miners' banners that features Sir Humphry Davy's lamp.

Unfortunately, the sad saga continued. Later that week workmen entered the Nova Scotia Pit, part of Harraton Colliery, to do repairs and did not return. A party was sent to seek them, but returned without the men because of chokedamp (also known as black damp where there was little oxygen and a high level of carbon dioxide) which had seeped into the pit because of the earlier explosion. Eight bodies were found the following day. Six men were dead and two were not expected to survive.

A cargo of coal and a closed hold could also be a lethal combination and spontaneous combustion of coal is a well known phenomenon even today.

The 'Fly'
July 4th, 1817

The 'Fly' from Ely, had just taken on coals from Mr Brandling's staithe on the River Tyne. The ship's hatches were closed at 8 pm and by 11.30 pm the master was writing by candlelight.

Coal may emit methane, a flammable gas. An air and methane mix between 5% and 16% methane can constitute an explosive atmosphere which may be ignited by sparks or a naked flame. The candle flame appears to have ignited. There was an explosion bursting the hatches open, throwing a boat resting on them into the air and ripping two planks off the deck! The master was scorched and his bedroom curtains were set alight. The mate was flung out of bed with his whiskers singed off and his toes burnt. The poor ship's cat was also singed and left without whiskers. Blame was directed at whoever gave the order to fasten down the hatches on fresh coals, thus allowing gas to build up in a confined, airless space.

Being out in countryside in bad weather could also be extremely dangerous.

A Flash in the Can
August 12th, 1831

Mr Edward Young, a farmer from near Ravensworth Castle, was shooting with a friend. Young primed his gun from a tin container during a thunderstorm. A flash of lightning caused the contents of the canister to explode and the gun went off. Both men were severely bruised and burnt.

Chemicals could also be dangerous indoors as one veterinary surgeon found to his cost.

A Dangerous Mix
May 30th, 1833

Mr Adamson, a veterinary surgeon in Durham, must have concocted medicines for animals every day of his life. Perhaps it was such a part of his routine that he forgot to think about the dangers when using chemicals. He poured coal tar and nitric acid into a quart bottle. Gas collected and the bottle exploded.

Not only was Mr Adamson wounded in his side by a shard of glass, but a servant outside was hurled against a wall and a horse was wounded in its thigh.

It would have been expected that a veterinary surgeon stored chemicals on his premises. However, who would expect to find explosives in the centre of Newcastle?

An Error of Judgement
December 17th, 1867

Police found nitroglycerin tucked away in the cellar of the White Swan Yard's in Newcastle's Cloth Market. Eight out of the nine canisters were in baskets. This discrepancy should, perhaps, have warned them that the explosive was in a very unstable state.

Nitroglycerin was synthesized in 1847 by Italian chemist Ascanio Sobrero and after gunpowder was the most powerful explosive then produced. It was oily, colourless and heavy. Physical shock could cause it to explode. After time, it can degrade and become even more unstable. Sobrero called it pyroglycerine and warned against its explosive properties.

Pyroglycerine became known as nitroglycerin and was first used commercially by Alfred Nobel, founder of 'Alfred Nobel & Company' in Germany. It was employed in the mining, construction and demolition industries and numerous catastrophes followed.

Newcastle's police had two choices: to explode the nitroglycerin where it was stored or transport it to a safer place. After discussing their dilemma with the town clerk and the magistrates, they decided to contact the Railway Company. Not surprisingly, the company wanted nothing to do with it.

The authorities were not to be thwarted. Someone made the decision that the nitroglycerin would be transported on a horse and cart through Newcastle to the Town Moor by Mr Mawson, the sheriff and Mr Bryson, the town surveyor. The idea being that the contents of the canisters would be emptied on the moor where there was subsidence caused by Spital Tongues Colliery. Soil would then be piled on top.

When they were on the way to the moor, John Mawson stopped the cart and examined the canisters so he would know how to open them once they reached their destination. A crowd gathered and followed them to the moor.

On arrival, the canisters were lifted down and placed on the grass. Mawson and Bryson told cartman Mr Appelby, employed by Hudson's provision merchant at the Cloth Market; labourer Mr Shotton from White Swan Yard; Sub-Inspector Wallace and PC 34A Donald Bain to '*draw the corks*' by using a pricker. Bryson drew several. The contents were poured out, but three canisters were still heavy.

John Mawson.

Mawson directed the men to strike off the ends of the canisters with a shovel. When this was done it was found that the nitroglycerin had crystallised and *'stuck to the tin'*.

'Bring them away and we will bury them on the other hill,' said Mawson. He then instructed Sub-Inspector Wallace to put soil on the liquid on the ground. Whilst Wallace did this, Appelby, Bain, Bryson, Shotton and the sheriff took the three canisters to the hill to bury them.

No one knows what happened. Perhaps one of the canisters was dropped, but there was a huge explosion sending out a shock wave travelling at thirty times the speed of sound. A white hot gas would have raised the temperature to about 5,000 degrees centigrade (9,030 degrees farenheit). Wallace was unbelievably lucky. The earth shook under his feet, but he was not hurt, probably because of a bank between him and the explosion. He reported seeing *'clothing and other articles fly up into the air.'*

One can only imagine Wallace's feelings as he raced to the west side of the hill to be greeted by a scene of utter devastation. Parts of PC Bain's *'mutilated and shattered body, other portions having been blown away'* were strewn in front of him. The mutilated bodies of Thomas Appelby and Shotton lay on the south side of the hill. A boy, Samuel Bell Wardley lay badly injured and close to death in a hole. Bryson was *'severely injured'* and lay to the east on the side bank and an injured Mawson was on top of the bank. George Smith Stonehouse, the young son of a clockmaker, and an unidentified man about 5ft 6 inches tall and about forty years old died at the scene. It was carnage!

Wallace tried to help Bryson, but he could not speak. Mawson was able to sit up. Desperate to get medical aid to these men and the boy, Wallace commandeered the cab which had brought Bryson and Mawson to the moor. Though 100 yards from the explosion, the blast had broken

The scene on the Town Moor.

the cab's windows and lifted the driver, Roxburgh, off his seat and onto his horses. He had seen one canister and clothing as they were flung high into the air.

Mr Walpole, a resident surgeon at the Infirmary, was walking on the moor as the explosion occurred. To his horror fragments of clothing, stone, dust and other debris rained down around him. As he approached the centre of the disaster three hundred yards away he found amongst other things, pieces of clothing, human flesh and a human foot possibly belonging to Bains. Bryson was a *'ghastly spectacle'* according to Walpole. Nevertheless, though Bryson appeared dead, Walpole attempted to save him by applying *'stimulants'*. The cart which had been used to transport the nitroglycerin was used to carry Bryson, Mawson and the boy, Samuel Wardley. Samuel, just a spectator, died within two hours of arriving at the Infirmary. Bryson and Mawson died the next night. In total eight people lost their lives.

An inquest was held on Mr Mawson as he was sheriff and basically in charge. The jury at the inquest returned this verdict:

'That death has been caused by the explosion of nitro-glycerine accidentally; and the jury are of the unanimous opinion that the law in reference to the storing of nitro-glycerine has been grossly violated in this case.' (Fordyce & Sykes, Vol. IV, p.5.)

Nothing was mentioned about the disastrous idea to transport an unstable, degraded explosive on a rickety cart through a crowded city centre or that crowds were allowed to follow and be spectators.

On a final ironic note, Alfred Nobel, who'd first used nitroglycerin commercially as an explosive, was treated with it for his heart complaint. It was used by doctors, in a diluted form, under the name Trintrin.

After railways were invented, and speed, heavy metal, steam and passengers were combined, accidents were to be expected. The next three accounts relate some of them:

Railway Accidents

The Clarence Railway Accident
March 19th, 1839

There was an accident on the Clarence Railway as a train going from Crowtrees to Stockton tried to round the bend on Mainsforth Carrs, near Middleham. The engine was hurled off the tracks and over the embankment. The passengers were unharmed, but the guard, fireman and engineman were killed when the engine rolled on top of them.

The Madness of a Moment
June 18th, 1840

A first class train from Stockton was due to arrive at a railway crossing, near Darlington, at any moment. The crossing gates were closed and the train was in sight as it sounded its whistle. These safety precautions did not appear to matter to a man called Prest. He was driving a loaded wagon on the Turnpike Road towards the crossing.

The guard at the gate attempted to stop Prest going further, but he pushed on through. He was half way across when the train hit and killed three of his horses, wrecked the wagon and sent timber everywhere. Amazingly the men on the engine, the passengers and Prest survived.

The opening of the Stockton to Darlington Railway.

January 22nd, 1870

Twenty six year old Bannon O'Neil was an impatient man. He took a risk when trying to cross the railway at Stockton when the gates were closed. Unfortunately he was struck by the train and carried several yards before falling with his head on the rail. He was decapitated.

O'Neil did not avoid his fate, though many prisoners tried to escape theirs over the centuries as several accounts below reveal.

Great Escapes

Prisons were supposedly built to keep prisoners in. When one man escaped it was probably thought unfortunate, but when several followed suit the authorities appear to have been at fault.

Getting to the Bottom of it ... Twice
August 1st, 1648

One night seventeen prisoners, escaped at night from Westgate Prison, Newcastle during a storm. Numerous visitors had apparently smuggled ropes to them which they had used to climb out of a privy.

At the same time six important prisoners also escaped from Tynemouth Castle by knotting sheets together and lowering themselves from the privy.

Escaping was not the sole prerogative of men. Gaols had their fair share of female escapees.

Woman Gang Member Escapes
August 24th, 1754

Elizabeth Rochester, a member of a gang of Faws (strolling pillagers or spoilers) escaped from Durham Gaol.

Although we do not know how Rochester escaped, prisoners' ingenuity knew no bounds.

Entrance Gate Newcastle Gaol

Pass the Hacksaw
August 15th, 1787

Four prisoners sawed off their irons and broke through the bars which enclosed the entrance to the privy on the east side of Newcastle Gaol. They escaped before any alarm was sounded.

Left: Newcastle Gaol was designed by John Dobson, built in 1823 and situated to the west of Carliol Square.

James Robinson did not need a hacksaw.

The Hole in the Wall Man
March 25th, 1841

James Robinson was a joiner. He had been held in Stockton's lock-up to face charges for a number of felonies. Having pulled the fireplace from the wall, he used one of the iron bars to create a hole and walked out.

Sometimes escaping gaol was not as simple as that, but Mary O'Neil managed it.

A Rope Trick
July 17th, 1870

Mary O'Neil was 27 years old, married and at the June sessions had been convicted of stealing a purse containing 12 shillings from a pitman's wife. Sentenced to seven years penal servitude, O'Neil said, *'Thank you; that's not nice. It'll do me no good. I'll come back as ever.'*

She was removed from the dock to a temporary cell and her cries and screams of, *"Murder"* interrupted the court proceedings. The court was cleared and she was taken by cab to Newcastle Gaol.

Placed in a cell at the northwest end of the prison, Mary broke an iron bar from her window and reached the wash house. She climbed out of the window and onto the roof which was almost the height of the prison wall. By fastening a rope to the wash house roof she got over the 25 ft boundary wall just above the gaol's entrance.

The rope was not long enough and O'Neil must have been left dangling in space before she dropped to the ground below. Unless she had an accomplice with a cart to cushion her fall, it is thought she must have injured herself. However, she got away.

Of course the numbers of those who escaped have to be weighed against those who did not, starting with a king.

Not So Great Escapes

King Caught!
May 13th, 1646

Towards the end of the Civil War, Charles I became a fugitive and eventually surrendered to the Scottish army at Newark-upon-Trent. He was taken to Newcastle upon Tyne where he was welcomed by a line of pikes, muskets, the sounds of drums, pealing bells and a guard of 300 Scots.

Lodged at the general's quarters, later the home of Major George Anderson, the king and his men were allowed out to walk and play *'goff'* (golf) on Shield Field.

Chambers, in his 'History of the Rebellions of Scotland 1638-60' quoted from a Sutherland family memoir that Robert Leslie, brother of Lieutenant-general Leslie, carried letters from the king to the Marquis of Huntly. Charles had written that once he was free he would meet Huntly in northern Scotland and warned him to have forces ready.

It is thought the king tried to escape along the Lort Burn which ran through the centre of Newcastle. He got as far as the middle of the Side where he was caught trying to get through an iron gate to a ship at the quay side.

With guards inside and outside his bedroom, Charles' days were numbered. He was eventually taken to London and executed at Whitehall on January 30th, 1649.
(*Sykes, Vol.I, p.99-100.*)

Some of those escaping did not care who was hurt in the process.

Turnkey Floored
June 15th 1789

Several prisoners attempted to escape from Morpeth Gaol. They sawed off their irons, broke an inner prison door and knocked a turnkey to the floor. On finding their way barred they took the turnkey prisoner and locked the door of their cell. The guards called for assistance from a *'party of artillery'* who were in the town and the escaping prisoners were overcome.
(*Sykes, Vol. I, p.350.*)

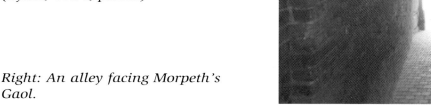

Right: An alley facing Morpeth's Gaol.

The thought of transportation sometimes drove prisoners to do desperate things.

Gaol Birds Caught
August 21st, 1789

Two prisoners, sentenced to transportation, attempted to escape from Newcastle Gaol by lowering themselves by rope on the east side of the prison. One sprained his leg and was captured on the same day at Gallowgate and the other was caught at Manor Chase. If these prisoners had successfully escaped from gaol, they would have found it almost impossible to escape the misery of their former lives. Those who had not broken the law, but were working in mines were also trapped having 'signed' the notorious Bond which basically enslaved them and members of their family.

Trouble at Mines

Coal wagon, Whitburn Collery.

The 1831 Strike

In 1830 Durham and Northumberland pitmen wanted one voice to represent huge numbers, so they formed one union, the Northern Union of Pitmen of Tyne and Wear or 'Hepburn's Union' (after leader Thomas Hepburn). They sought to improve the conditions they worked under, such as the annual bond which legally contracted them to work in a pit for a year, the working hours of boys and the 'Tommy Shop' where miners received tommy checks instead of wages. (This meant they were forced to buy goods at inflated prices from a relative or viewer of the colliery. If a miner was in arrears, his pay would be confiscated and the balance given to the shopkeeper).

Conditions underground were difficult and highly dangerous. For example Durham Mining Museum records a series of disasters at Jarrow Colliery (also known as the Temple Main Colliery or less officially as the 'fiery pit' or the 'slaughter house'). The reason for the last two nicknames can be seen in the pit's disastrous safety record in the early 19th century.

Jarrow Colliery Disasters

January 25th, 1817	6 dead.
January 17th, 1826	34 dead.
March 15th, 1828	8 dead.
August 3rd, 1830	42 dead.
August 21st, 1845	39 dead.

Jarrow Colliery was only one pit amongst many in which it was obvious safety lessons were not being learnt quickly enough in the relentless drive, regardless of the cost in human lives, to put money into the pit owners' pockets.

In 1831-32 a number of key events occurred. There was a campaign for parliamentary reform, the economy slumped and a cholera epidemic was raging. Matters were brought to a head in a series of bitter clashes between miners and mine owners in Northumberland and Durham during the 1831 Great Strike. It is against this backcloth that the miners, their employers and government should be judged

The owners appeared to have the backing of the government, local magistrates and the militia. The miners were determined to have the backing of the general public. The strike lasted until September 1831. At least one concession was gained: the reduction of working hours for boys from 16 hours to 12 hours. This is what happened:

Jarrow Colliery (1803-1934).

March 21st, 1831

Miners from 47 collieries in Tyne and Wear peacefully marched through Newcastle and by 1 pm 120,000 men held a meeting on the Town Moor to improve their conditions. Their grievances lay in parts of the Bond of service. The miners objected to being laid off with no wages for three days when a minor accident occurred at the pit, engines or wagon railroads. They also felt it wrong that boys should work for such long hours to the detriment of their health, education and morals. The viewer was also thought to have too much control over continuous work and pit housing and families could be evicted on completion of work or for not fulfilling some articles of the Bond.

At the meeting the miners collected 6d from each pitman so they could send representatives to London to petition Parliament. They decided that when they completed this employment period, they would work without a Bond, if the owners agreed. If not, the miners would strike and claim parish relief or ask magistrates to act on their behalf. The miners were determined their demands would be met and that they would meet twice a week to which delegates from each pit would be sent. No miner would now buy meat, drink or candles from anyone who had anything to do with the mines.

The meeting ended with the miners thanking the Mayor of Newcastle, Archibald Reed, Esq who offered to mediate between the men and their employers. He also advised them to be peaceful as this was the best means of obtaining justice for their cause.

March 31st, 1831

Miners from Tyne and Wear collieries held a meeting on Black Fell, County Durham to demand higher wages.

April 5th, 1831

This was the day the annual Bond ended for the Tyne and Wear miners and they refused to sign the next one until their demands were met. The employers agreed wages should be paid in money, that the miners could purchase goods where they pleased and that boys would have a shorter working day. However, the miners insisted that all their conditions were addressed.

April 6th, 1831

There was another meeting of miners at Black Fell in the hope their employers would concede to their demands. This did not happen. The military was placed in a state of readiness and several magistrates with no connections with the collieries offered their services as mediators to no avail.

April 18th, 1831

Blyth and Bedlington collieries found themselves besieged by 1,200 to 1,500 miners who threatened to set fire to the pits unless work was stopped. Tempers rose and at Bedlington Glebe pit, machinery was damaged, corves (a small engine for carrying coal or a wicker-work basket containing 7-8 cwt of coal) were torn to pieces and thrown down the shaft. The miners were stopped at Netherton when they were given ale.

There was also trouble at pits on the River Wear. Miners had threatened to '*murder the horse-keepers if they went down the pit to attend the horses.*'

The authorities were very concerned. Not only were special constables, the Northumberland and Newcastle Yeomanry and some of the 82nd regiment in Sunderland called out, but also 80 marines and three subalterns from Portsmouth. (*Sykes Vol. II, p.297.*)

Meetings were held at Black Fell, Boldon Colliery and Friars Goose and Gateshead.

April 21st, 1831

Tyne and Wear pitmen waving banners from 49 collieries met in Jarrow. The men agreed to '*adhere to their former resolutions*'. Perhaps the mood of the meeting can be judged by the fact that various speakers pleaded for the men be orderly and to keep the peace. (*Sykes, Vol. II, p.298.*)

Boldon Colliery (1866-1982).

May 5th, 1831

A large group of miners met at Black Fell where they were asked to disperse by the Marquis of Londonderry and his military escort. He offered to meet the miners' delegates at the Coal Trade office, Westgate Street, Newcastle. This was agreed, but the meeting failed to solve the miners' demands. There was a second meeting the same day, where the owners offered terms, but they were unacceptable to the miners.

Most of the collieries, bar two or three which had military protection, had stopped working and the country was now desperate for coal. The striking miners would have been desperate for their wages to pay bills, rent and feed their families. Tensions were rising.

The government increased the military's profile in the area. Colonel Bell's dismounted troops and cavalry were stationed near Wallsend where they supported detachments of regulars (horse and foot). Collieries had sentries protecting men at work and engines. Apparently '*squadrons of cavalry scoured the countryside for idle men looking for trouble*'. Despite Thomas Hepburn's pleas to be peaceful, there were numerous battles between the militia and pitmen. Many pitmen and their families were starving, homeless and forced to beg all over Durham and Northumberland. The strike ended in a victory for the miners in June, 1831 and perhaps did not come soon enough for some miners' families. (*Sykes,Vol. II, p. 299.*)

Nine miners who worked at Jarrow Collliery committed a crime on the April 29th, 1831 and the authorities perhaps with memories of the American Revolution 1763-87; horror of the French Revolution 1789-1802; Napoleon Bonaparte having waged war on Europe from 1803-15 and the recent miners' strike still fresh in their minds, used the full weight of the law against the miscreants. The unfairness of their sentence was to reverberate through the centuries.

The nine men were: Thomas Armstrong (23), John Barker (25), Isaac Eccleston (23), David Johnson (25), Thomas Pringle, Thomas Kenare, John Smith (24), John Stewart (26) and Bartholomew Stephenson (18). They were apprehended and taken before Mr Fairles, a magistrate, charged with house breaking and sent to gaol to await trial. Kenare and Pringle escaped, but the remaining seven were tried at the Durham and Sadberge Assizes. John Barker was tried for stealing guns.

There is an account of their trial in 'The Durham County Advertiser', Friday 29th, July 1831. This is what happened. The men were *'severally charged with having, at Hedworth, feloniously entered the dwelling-house of Thomas Jewett and demanded money and meat; and also violently assaulting and ill-treating him; and also with feloniously stealing from the dwelling-house of the said Thomas Jewett, two guns, his property.'*

Thomas Jewett was called to the witness stand by Mr Bainbridge. Jewett lived *'at Hedworth, in the parish of Jarrow'* and was in bed at 8 pm on April 29th, when a servant called him between eight and nine o'clock. He found two men in his house. When asked what they wanted they replied *'bread, meat, money and bacon.'* Jewett did not know who they were. One of the men went out and *' ... brought in the rest.'* Jewett said he *' ... gave them a shilling; they demanded more, and forced another shilling out of my hand which my wife had given me; they also took two guns out of the house. One of them struck my wife on the face, when she fell down on the ground and the blood came out of her ear. They struck me also on the face, and I fell against the dresser quite stupefied. My wife has been ill ever since with fright. I am sure the men at the bar are the same that were in my house.'*

The next witness was Mary Jewett, Thomas Jewett's granddaughter who also lived in Hedworth. She said she had met two of the men as she was leaving her grandfather's house. Her grandmother was in the room and the men *'asked for some bacon, bread, and eighteen-pence.'* When her grandmother refused to give them anything, they said *'they would fetch their gang.'* She called for her grandfather and was sent out of the house to fetch her uncle Thomas. By the time she got back at 10 pm there were only her uncle, grandfather and grandmother in the house.

'Thomas Jewett the younger' (Mary's uncle) gave his account. He said when he arrived at the house he found his father (Thomas Jewett) *'bleeding from the mouth'* and his mother *'from the ear'*. He also said five of the perpetrators returned the following day asking to see his father *'and if he had gone to get warrants for them.'* Thomas told them his father was in Shields. *'They said they were sorry for what they done, and that they would return the guns and every expense.'* Thomas told them he would *'endeavour to prevail on my father to make it up with them. They then went away.'*

Two publicans were also called as witnesses. Thomas Robinson stated that the prisoners had all been drinking in his premises from 3 pm till 9 pm on April 29th. John Rowell said he knew Armstrong, Stewart, Smith and Johnson and that they were at his premises between 9 pm to 10 pm on this night. A man had come in and said *'Lads, we are called on.'* All the men left. There is some confusion in this evidence. Could the Jarrow men have been in different places at 9 pm? Were the publicans lying?

The 'Royal Oak' also known as the 'Long Bar' is a typical public house in Jarrow and stands on the corner of Staple Road and Grange Road.

Could Jewett be absolutely sure all the seven men in the dock were those who broke into his house? It seems odd that none of the men wore masks either during or after the crime. Jewett said the men were in his house between 8 and 9 pm. Mary Jewett said she returned to the house and the men were no longer there at 'about ten o'clock.'

It is interesting the older Jewett used the word 'demanded' when commenting on the manner in which he was addressed by the men, and his granddaughter used the word 'asked'. Were the men merely begging for sustenance for their families, but affronted by Jewett's tone and perhaps ignorance of their economic plight, decided to go one step too far in the excitement and drama of the moment?

There is no doubt that the men should not have been in Jewett's home and it was certainly threatening behaviour for the first two miners to bring seven more strange men into the house. However, no one was murdered, and the older Jewett and his wife were 'struck' by only one or possibly two out of the nine men. Yet all nine men were arrested and would have all been put on trial, if two, Kenare and Pringle had not escaped.

The men wanted a paltry amount of money and food. At worst a little blood was spilled and two guns were taken at a time when the authorities were having problems with miners and the militia were being called.

The first twist in the tale is that five of the men returned the following day to apologise to the older Thomas Jewett, which must be the most unusual recorded criminal behaviour from any time. Had the men slept on what they had done and suddenly realised this was a serious crime and they might face the death penalty? Had they been prevailed upon by family and friends to do the right thing and make amends?

Under the Bloody Code they were found guilty and initially sentenced to death, though ' ... it was intimated to the prisoners that they would be transported for seven years.' Was the first sentence of death an overreaction by the judge? Was it meant to be a lesson to the rest of the troublesome miners who had the temerity to take on the pit owners and strike for improved pay and conditions? Were the authorities concerned about a revolution? The second twist in the men's tale was that though the sentence was mercifully commuted to transportation on July 23rd, 1831, it was not for seven years, but for life. (*Newcastle Courant, July 29th, 1831.*)

In 1717 the Transportation Act gave judges an alternative punishment to death and in some circumstances made transportation a punishment in its own right. Between the years 1788-1842 about 80,000 convicts were shipped to New South Wales, Australia. 85% were men and 15% women. The majority were first offenders convicted for receiving stolen goods or petty larceny.

Convicts were then taken south to gaol or a hulk to await embarkation. These men were apparently sent to Woolwich and (according to Bartholomew Stephenson's descendants) held on the hulk 'Justitia'. They would have had a haphazard medical examination, as many suffered numerous diseases because of the length of time of their incarceration. Two sets of footwear and clothing would have been issued prior to their boarding the 'Isabella I' for transportation to New South Wales, Australia – a 13,000 mile journey.

The hulk 'Justitia'.

84

Transportation

'The Voyage'

'All of you that's in England and live at home in ease,
Be warned by us poor lad, forc'd to cross the seas
That are forced to cross the seas among the savages to go,
To leave friends and relations to work at the hoe.' (Anon).

The 'Isabella I' left London, called in at Woolwich and finally departed from Plymouth for New South Wales captained by William Wiseman on November 27th, 1831. Apparently a soldier overheard some convicts plotting to take the ship if the opportunity arose. Fifty-two year old Surgeon Superintendent, Thomas Galloway ensured the convicts were confined in double irons for some time afterwards.

Galloway kept a detailed diary of the voyage. There was a lot of illness which he thought was due to a change of habits and diet. Sea sickness predominated until they rounded the Cape of Good Hope and were enveloped in fog. After this any sickness became severe and lingered on.

Private contractors were in charge of transportation and there was no economic benefit in ensuring the prisoners were fit and healthy on arrival and the dead could not protest. Provisions were usually of good quality, but meagre as profit could be made from serving less. Captain Wiseman was part owner of the 'Isabella I'.

On February 6th, 1832 events took a dramatic turn when the ship was 350 leagues (1690 km) off the south east Coast of Madagascar. Second mate Bourne ordered sailor Jacob Anderson to hang up a clothes line for the convicts. He and the crew refused to work. Anderson was ordered to the poop, but did not remain there.

The 'Isabella I'.

Some of the crew began to push the chief mate when he tried to grab Anderson. Eventually Anderson was seized and put on the poop in irons. The crew hissed, hooted, refused to work and a sailor, John Payne, left the wheel. One sailor apparently said, *'Fire away, we can stand it.'* The guard ran on deck, but the sailors tried to persuade them to stay out of it. One soldier shouted that he did not like being flogged and *'Hurrah for the sailors!'* Captain Clark of the 4th regiment ordered the man flogged immediately.

The sailors who mutinied were put in irons that night away from the convicts. Next morning nine sailors returned to their posts, but one, Griffiths, was clasped in irons again because he wanted all of the sailors released. The sailors were in irons from February 6th to March 15th, 1832. The ship was navigated by officers, seamen who obeyed orders, boys, soldiers and convicts.

After approximately four months at sea, the 'Isabella I' arrived in New South Wales, Australia on the March 15th, 1832 having transported 226 male convicts, two died on the voyage; a crew of 45 men and the guard, the 4th regiment, consisting of 38 privates and non-commissioned officers, four women and nine children.

In the ensuing court case the seamen were found guilty of revolt. It was later reported when brought before Judge Dowling, they were told off, discharged, ordered to pay £100 each to keep the peace for twelve months and pardoned.

New South Wales, Australia

So what happened to the seven miners from Jarrow once they arrived in New South Wales? They appear to have been assigned to the Australian Agricultural Company (AAC). The area was described by Roger Dawson, who was appointed the chief agent for the AAC in 1824, '*Nothing can be more salubrious, or more delightful than the climate of New South Wales, in every quarter which I have visited. The richness of some part of the soil in the numerous valleys and, the beauty of the scenery in those places, can hardly in my imagination, be exceeded in any part of the world.*' He went on to say that he knew '*of no country in the world more calculated, as regards climate and situation, for human enjoyment.*'

Of course he was viewing NSW from the perspective of a free man who was financially solvent, not from the jaundiced and homesick viewpoint of a transported convict who was not. At first the men may have thought they would have an easy time of it, working on the land instead of below it.

In 1824 the AAC was incorporated and, with the agreement of the British Government was told to select one million acres of prime land in New South Wales with some conditions attached. A Court of Directors was appointed with an advisory colonial committee. The committee was in charge of expenditure and appointed an agent answerable to them. Port Stephens was finally chosen by the company.

The company's aims were to produce good quality wool and some crops not available in England. This would mean a large number of convicts would be employed producing goods at no cost to the British Government.

However, by the 1820s the company was granted an additional 2,000 acres at Newcastle to develop coal mines. In 1830 the government gave the company the Newcastle Coal works and by 1831 the mine was operational, but required miners. Free convict labour would have been highly desirable and the Jarrow miners arrived at this time.

It is probable that the Jarrow miners were not agricultural workers or shepherds and that there was to be no escape from life at a coal seam for them. The irony of the town's name, Newcastle, and the origins of the steam engine pumping water, made by Messrs Hawthorne of Newcastle upon Tyne, could not have been missed by the Jarrow miners. Nor the fact that instead of striking for better pay and working conditions in the North East of England, some if not all were now labouring in an Australian mine with no rights at all.

Jarrow Hall was built by Simon Temple and is a Grade II listed building. Temple was the owner of Jarrow Colliery (Temple Main Pit) which he opened in 1803.

The Jarrow miners' records are below:

Thomas Armstrong

Born: About 1807.
Age: 24.
Religion: Protestant.
Children: –
Trade or Calling: Miner.
Trial: Durham and Sadberge Assizes.
Sentence: Life.
Height: 5' 7^1/$_2$''.
Hair: Dark brown.

Arrival: Mar 15th, 1832 at Sydney Cove, NSW.
Education: None.
Married/Single: Single.
Native place: Durham.
Offence: Housebreaking.
Trial date: July 23rd, 1831.
Previous Convictions: None.
Complexion: Dark sallow.
Eyes: Dark hazel.

Particular Marks or Scars. Remarks: Scar over left brow, scar on right cheek, blue scar over right eyebrow. Bird upper, 'MAEASAGA' on lower right arm. Woman and several letters on lower left.

This is probably what happened to him:

The gaol records show Armstrong may well have been arrested for drunkenness on two occasions and once for indecent language when he had to pay a fine of a £1 or spend 7 days in the cells.

December 1835: Charged with robbing Sarah Sharrod in Newcastle, New South Wales. Discharged from court.

February 1836: Charged with drunkenness and disorderly conduct at Newcastle, NSW. Arrested by Constable Rouse and sentenced to 50 lashes.

Record: June 10th, 1840: Ticket of leave holder. District: Newcastle, NSW.

Death: February, 22nd, 1844. District: Newcastle, NSW.

According to one Australian source, Armstrong's brother, Ralph in Jarrow, was so incensed that Thomas had been transported he later murdered Mr Fairles, the magistrate who committed the seven men to trial. Unfortunately, Ralph's accomplice, William Jobling, who held Fairles' horse, was hanged and gibbeted for the crime on Jarrow Slake, near St Paul's monastery. Ralph escaped and was never heard of again. It is rumoured that Ralph fled to Australia and Jobling's fate is widely regarded as a gross injustice in Jarrow today.

Above: An etching of William Jobling, Ralph Armstrong's accomplice.

Left: The slake, where William Jobling was gibbeted, lies on the far side of this old stone bridge, near St Paul's Church in Jarrow.

St Paul's, an Anglo-Saxon church in Jarrow, has the oldest dedication stone in England, AD 685.

John Barker

Born: About 1806.   **Age:** 26.
Education: Reading.   **Religion:** Protestant.
Married/Single: Single.   **Children:** –
Native Place: Durham.   **Trade or Calling:** Miner.
Offence: Stealing gun. (The 'Durham County Advertiser' stated he stole two guns).
Trial: Durham and Sadberge.   **Trial date:** July 23rd, 1831.
Sentence: Life.   **Previous Convictions:** None.
Height: 5' 3$^{1}/_{2}$".   **Complexion:** Sallow.
Hair: Brown.   **Eyes:** Grey.
Particular Marks or Scars. Remarks: Blue mark near both eyes, scar on left side of forehead.

This is probably what happened to him:

1837: Assigned to the Australian Agricultural Company in Newcastle, NSW.

Witness: Campbell/Grayson case.

Record: 1844: Ticket of leave holder.

District: Port Stephens; Tried: Durham Saelberg (sic).

December 11th, 1847: Conditional Pardon at age 41 years.

Only one John Barker married in the general area of the Hunter region, near Newcastle at this time. If this was him, his bride was Lettitia Noyes.

Isaac Eccleston
(Also recorded as Eccliston/Ecclestone/Eggleton/Egglestone/Heckleson)

Born: About 1809.
Education: Reading & Writing.
Married/Single: Single.
Native Place: Northumberland.
Offence: Housebreaking.
Trial date: July 23rd, 1831.
Former Convictions: None.
Complexion: Sallow and freckled.
Eyes: Dark grey.

Age: 24.
Religion: Protestant.
Children: –
Trade or Calling: Miner.
Trial: Durham and Sadberge Assizes.
Sentence: Life.
Height: 5' 5$^{1}/_{2}$''.
Hair: Dark brown.

Particular Marks or Scars. Remarks: Scar on left cheek bone, '6th July 1831', and woman on lower right arm. Fish 'IE DC STF' on lower left arm.

This is probably what happened to him:

January 1832: Assigned Australian Agricultural Company (AAC) at Port Stephens, NSW.

1837: Assigned AAC.

1840: Record: Ticket of Leave holder for the Newcastle district, NSW.

June 1840: Still in the Newcastle area.

1842: Moved to Maitland area.

1843: Recommended for a Ticket of Leave, for Newcastle district.

1843: Ticket holder when granted permission to marry Ann Clark (she came free on the ship 'Agnes Ewing') in the district of Maitland.

1846: Recommended for a Conditional Pardon.

1846: Received Conditional Pardon.

September 8th, 1847: Received Conditional Pardon.

April 5th, 1853: Isaac, a former miner, appears to have changed his name to Eggleston*. He purchased two quarter acre lots (4 and 5) costing £99 in Blane Street, Newcastle at the Australian Agriculture Company's auction.

*Convicts often altered or changed their names to hide their criminal background

A sketch of Botany Bay – the most famous destination for convicts.

David Johnson

Born: About 1807.
Education: None.
Married/Single: Single.
Native Place: Northumberland.
Offence: Housebreaking.
Trial date: July 23rd, 1831.
Former Convictions: None.
Complexion: Ruddy freckled.
Eyes: Grey.

Age: 25.
Religion: Protestant.
Children: –
Trade or Calling: Miner.
Trial: Durham and Sadberge.
Sentence: Life.
Height: 5' 7''.
Hair: Sandy.

Particular Marks or Scars. Remarks: Scum on right eye, red whiskers. Satan (sic) on lower right arm. Woman, fish, and other figures on lower left arm.

Records reveal a David Johnson with similar tattoos in and out of gaol in 1854, 1861, 1865, 1868 and 1870. His crimes appear to range from drunkenness, to discharging *'belan/se'* in an unauthorised place, to refusing to pay his steamer fare. His punishments ranged from 1-3 months hard labour to a fine of £20.

This is probably what happened to him:

1835: Assigned to the Australian Agricultural Company, NSW.

Remanded for further evidence after being charged with robbing Sharon Sharrod while in church in Newcastle, NSW.

1843: Assigned to the Australian Agricultural Company.

Sentenced to two months hard labour for disorderly conduct in Newcastle, NSW.

1847: Ticket of Leave holder. District: Newcastle and Murrundi, NSW.

John Smith

Born: About 1808.
Education: Reading & Writing.
Married/Single: Single.
Native Place: Durham.
Offence: Housebreaking.
Trial date: July 23rd, 1831.
Former Convictions: None.
Complexion: Dark sallow.
Eyes: Dark grey.

Age: 24.
Religion: Protestant.
Children: –
Trade or Calling: Miner.
Trial: Durham and Sadberge Assizes.
Sentence: Life.
Height: 5' 7''.
Hair: Dark brown.

Particular Marks or Scars. Remarks: Large scar on right eyebrow. Woman, 'WSJS' on lower right arm. 'REWETSB', '1808', heart and two darts on lower left arm.

This is probably what happened to him:

1832: Assigned to the Australian Agricultural Company, NSW.

Charged with disorderly conduct in Newcastle, NSW.

December 1835: Assigned to the Australian Agricultural Company, NSW.

Sentenced to 75 lashes for drunkenness.

Record: Ticket of Leave holder. District: Newcastle, NSW.

November 1st, 1848: Conditional Pardon.

Bartholomew Stephenson

Born: July 11th, 1813, Jarrow.
Parents: Arthur Stephenson and Alice Todd. (Bartholomew's death certificate names his father as Rodger, but according to his descendants, Rodger was his brother).

Father's occupation: Blacksmith.
Age: 18.
Religion: Protestant.
Children: –
Trade or Calling: Miner.
Trial: Durham and Sadberge.
Sentence: Life.
Complexion: Sallow.
Hair: Brown.

Brothers: Arthur and Rodger.
Education: Reading.
Married/Single: Single.
Native Place: Durham.
Offence: Housebreaking.
Trial date: July 23rd, 1831.
Previous Convictions: None.
Height: 5' 3³/4".
Eyes: Grey.

Particular Marks or Scars. Remarks: Woman, anchor, 'JCBS' on lower right arm. Woman and anchor on lower left arm.

This is probably what happened to him:

1832: Assigned to the Australian Agricultural Company, NSW.

1844: Ticket of Leave granted. District: Newcastle, NSW.

July 30th, 1847: Conditional Pardon.

Stephenson was sent to Port Stephens, south of Newcastle and was still in NSW In 1835. On February 11th, 1842, he was 28 years of age, a resident in Newcastle and was arrested for drunkenness. He obtained a Conditional Pardon on July 30th, 1847 in Sydney, NSW and in 1855 married Christina Melville in a Church of England ceremony at St Andrew's, Sydney. This is now the Anglican Cathedral and very prestigious. Between the ages of 62-80, he lived in Ryde, NSW. After Christina's death he married her sister Mary in 1879 when he was 66 years of age. His nephew/son John Stephenson married another of the Melville sisters, Catherine.

In 1890 Bartholomew's residence was Tewitt's Road, North Ryde, between Langton Cove and Shrimpton Creek. He was a fruit grower as were all his neighbours. He may have had citrus orchards as Ryde is mainly clay and citrus fruits thrive in this soil. After living in the colony for 64 years and following an illness lasting six months, he died of '*Senile Decay*' at the age of 82 years on April 24th, 1894 and is buried in St Anne's Cemetery, Ryde. His occupation was noted as 'farmer' on his Death Certificate. There is no headstone to mark his resting place. Bartholomew never saw his parents again.

On a lighter note, according to Bartholomew's descendants, his nephew John Stephenson emigrated to Australia. The men undoubtedly met as it was John who was one of the witnesses at Bartholomew's burial. Also Arthur, Bartholomew's older brother, had a daughter Jane who married Edward Jameson and emigrated to Kansas, USA. Their son and granddaughter became well known illustrators in New York and had a very privileged childhood.

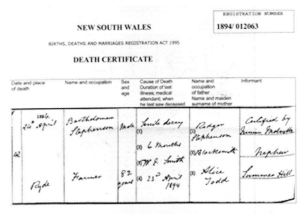

Stephenson's death certificate.
(*NSW Death Certificate 1894/012063*).

John Stewart/Steward

Born: About 1805. **Age:** 27.
Education: None. **Religion:** Protestant.
Married/Single: Single. **Children:** –
Native Place: Durham. **Trade or Calling:** Miner.
Offence: Housebreaking. **Trial:** Durham and Sadberge Assizes.
Trial date: July 23rd, 1831. **Former Convictions:** None.
Height: 5' 5¹/₂". **Complexion:** Dark sallow.
Hair: Dark brown. **Eyes:** Hazel.
Particular Marks or Scars. Remarks: Scar on left eyebrow. Lost a front tooth right upper side of jaw. Fish and several letters on lower left arm. Woman on lower right arm.

This is probably what happened to him:

1832: Assigned to the Australian Agricultural Company, NSW.

Record: Ticket of Leave, District: Newcastle, NSW.

July 30th, 1847: Conditional Pardon.

On July 26th, 1892, John Stewart committed bigamy in Wallsend, NSW.

It is interesting to note that all of the men were miners in their twenties and only one, Stephenson, was the tender age of eighteen. None had any previous convictions, were married or had children. Five were from Durham, two from Northumberland and they were all Protestants. Three had no formal education, two could read and write and two were only able to read. In the poverty and deprivation of the times, what chance did the semi-literate or illiterate have?

All of them, except for Stephenson, had scars and Armstrong and Barker had blue marks or scars, possibly from coal dust getting into a wound. They all had tattoos apart from Barker. Fish, a bird, anchors, letters, a date, a heart and two darts and women all feature. Perhaps the most notable tattoos are those on Johnson who has the word 'scum' on his right eye and worse 'satan' (sic) on an arm.

They all received life sentences for 'housebreaking' except Barker whose crime was 'stealing a gun'. None of them had any previous convictions. Was it the 1831 strike and hunger that drove them to commit this crime?

Jarrow continued to be a mining community for many years. Here are some typical miners' cottages and local men.

Convict discipline in Australia depended on punishments and rewards for good behaviour. Tickets of Leave and Conditional Pardons were part of a system of inducement to behave.

Tickets of Leave

First, convicts had to prove they were industrious, sober and honest. They applied through their master to a magistrate. Once they received their ticket they would have been regarded as elite workers. (There were exemptions for those who had influential friends in England or anyone who had been extremely heroic.) The ticket allowed the convicts the freedom to work for themselves and acquire land.

Those convicts given a life sentence, like the above men, would have usually needed to either serve eight years with one master, ten years with two or twelve years with three. There were stipulations. The convict had to carry the ticket with him at all times; to report regularly to the local authority; to stay in a specified area and if possible attend church every Sunday.

Conditional Pardons

A Conditional Pardon meant freedom with the stipulation that convicts could not return to '*the United Kingdom or Ireland*'.

The End of Transportation

The transportation of convicts to New South Wales was abolished on October 1st, 1850, though the last transport arrived at Freemantle on January 10th, 1868. Pressure from the eastern colonies combined with rising costs persuaded the British Government to put a stop to it.

There is one final twist in these men's stories. In May 1842, ten years after their convictions, even if they thought they had been forgotten by everyone they held dear in England, they had not. There was a petition for clemency signed by '*John Archer Forster (for Jarrow Colliery, employer) and undersigned by 16 inhabitants of Jarrow; Hugh Nanney, (vicar of Jarrow) undersigned by 85 inhabitants of Jarrow; Hugh Nanney.*' HRC Chaytor MP sent the petition to the Home Department.

A coin produced to mark the end of transportation.

The grounds given were of the men's youth, former good character and sobriety. It was argued the offence had been committed against the background of the strike and their former employer had agreed that if they returned they would have jobs. They also reasoned that justice had been satisfied as they had served ten years of their sentence with good behaviour. (Not perhaps correct in all cases.)

Unfortunately Lord Durham petitioned against mitigation on the grounds that their Jarrow employer had been intimidated when asked to sign the petition and that the punishment was correct. Lord Durham won and the seven men stayed in Australia for the rest of their lives.

We are left with one burning question, however: what happened to Kenare and Pringle?

Conclusion

If like me you were born in the North East, then you probably thirst to know more about its history. The past forewarns. It has left us a rich heritage forged by everyday life with all its inherent dangers, strange happenings and the furnace of war. It is amazing what our ancestors had to endure, wonder at and survive. I hope this book whets your appetite for more.

Lorna Windham
2014

Bibliography

Alexander, M. (2011). In Search of Britain's Haunted Castles, The History Press.

Anderson, M. (2005). Executions & Hangings in Newcastle & Morpeth, Wharncliffe Books, South Yorkshire.

Chambers, R. (1828). History of the Rebellions in Scotland (1638-1660).

Dawson, R. Esq, (1830). The Present State of Australia and Description of the Country, its Advantages and Prospects with reference to Emigration, and a particular Account of the Manners, Customs and Conditions of its Aboriginal Inhabitants, Smith, Elder, London.

Fordyce, T. & Sykes J. (1867). Vol. III & IV, Local Records; or, Historical register of remarkable events. T. Fordyce, Newcastle.

Gardiner, L. (1968). The British Admiralty, W. Blackwell & Sons, Edinburgh and London.

Hawthorne, P. (2001). Corunna 1809: Sir John Moore's Fighting Retreat, Osprey Publishing.

Hof, U.I. (1994). The Enlightenment, Blackwell, Oxford.

Knowles, M. (Not stated). The History of Jarrow, Halfway Tree Publications, Tyne and Wear.

Mackenzie & Dent. (1810). A Historical and Descriptive View of the County of Northumberland and of The Town and County of Newcastle upon Tyne with Berwick-upon-Tweed and other celebrated Places on the Scottish Border (Vol. II). Mackenzie and Dent, Newcastle.

Morgan, A. (2007). Victorian Panorama, City of Newcastle upon Tyne, Newcastle Libraries and Information Service, Tyne Bridge Publishing.

Pack, S.W.C. (1960). Admiral Lord Anson, Cassell & Co, London.

Paine, T. (1791 Part I, 1792 Part II). The Rights of Man.

Smith, K. and J. (2008). The Great Northern Miners, City of Newcastle upon Tyne Newcastle Libraries and & Information Service, Tyne Bridge Publishing.

Smith, K, Yellowley, T. (2012). The Great Walls of Newcastle, City of Newcastle upon Tyne Newcastle Libraries and & Information Service, Tyne Bridge Publishing.

Sykes, J. (1866). Vol. I &II, Local Records; of, Historical Events, Which have Occurred in Northumberland and Durham, Newcastle upon Tyne, and Berwick upon Tweed, From the Earliest Period of Authentic Record to the Present Time; with Biographical Notices of Deceased Persons of Talent, Eccentricity and Longevity, Vol. 1, II, T. Fordyce, Newcastle.

Watson, K. (2004). Poisoned Lives, English Poisoners and their Victims, Hambledom Continuum, London, New York.

Journals

Thomas Galloway's Journal, October 24th, 1831 – March 30th, 1832.

Criminal Registers

England and Wales Criminal Registers, 1791-1892.

UK, Prison Hulk Registers and Letter Book, 1802-1849.

Magazines

Mechanics' Magazine – Vol. XV, No. 395, March 5th, 1831.

Newspapers

Cumberland Chronicle

Daily News (London, England), Monday, March 1st, 1847; Issue 235.

Durham County Advertiser, Friday, July 29th, 1831.

Freeman's Journal and Daily commercial Advertiser (Dublin, Ireland), Saturday, March 20th, 1847; Issue N/A.

Hampshire Telegraph and Sussex Chronicle etc. (Portsmouth, England), Saturday, March 20th, 1847; Issue 2476.

Hull Packet and East Riding Times (Hull, England), Friday, March 26th, 1847; Issue 3244.

Ipswich Journal (Ipswich, England), Saturday, March 20th, 1847; Issue 5628.

Leeds Mercury, Saturday, October 16th, 1869

Leeds Mercury, Friday, November 22nd, 1872
Leeds Mercury, Friday, October 25th, 1872
Leeds Mercury, Wednesday, November 27th, 1872
Lloyds Evening-Post, Vol. XLII – Numb. 3252. Monday, April 27th, to Wednesday, April 29th, 1778.
Lloyds's Weekly London Newspaper (London, England) Sunday, October 18th, 1846; Issue 204.
Morning Chronicle (London, England), Monday, March 1st, 1847; Issue 24134.
Monthly Chronicle of North-country Lore and Legend, London.
Newcastle Courant, July 1st, 1831
Newcastle Courant, Saturday, July 30th, 1831.
Newcastle Courant, Friday March 5th, 1847; Issue 8987.
Newcastle Courant, Friday, December 17th, 1869
Newcastle Courant, October 18th, 1872
Newcastle Courant, November, 29th, 1872
Newcastle Courant, January 4th, 1878, p.1-2.
Newcastle Courant, January 25th, 1878.
Northern Echo, Monday, January 27th, 1873
The Era (London, England), Sunday, October 18th, 1846; Issue 421.
The Morning Chronicle (London, England), Monday, March 1st, 1847; Issue 24134.

Doctoral Thesis

Ridley, D. (1994). Political and industrial crisis: the experience of the Tyne and Wear pitmen, 1831-1832, Durham University.

Australian Sources

Ancestry Family Trees
Australia Death Index, 1787-1985 – Thomas Armstrong Citation: (4/4549; Reel: 690; Page: 605.)
Australia Marriage Index, 1788-1950
Port Stephens Family History Society Journal, Spring 2013
New South Wales and Tasmania, Australian Convict Musters, 1806-49
New South Wales, Australia Convict Ship Muster Rolls and Related Records, 1790-1849
New South Wales, Australia, Convict Indents, 1788-1842
New South Wales, Convict Registers of Conditional and Absolute Pardons, 1788-1870
State Archives, NSW, Kingswood, New South Wales; Gaol Description and Entrance Books, 1818-1930; Item: 2/2020; Roll: 757
New South Wales, Australia, Settler and Convict Lists, 1787-1834
Sands Directories (Printers and Stationers): Sydney New South Wales, Australia, 1858-1933; 1890; Part 4, p.411

Websites

www.jenwilletts.com
www.jenwilletts.com
www.dmm.org.uk
www.nationalarchives.gov.uk
www.royalnavalmuseum.org
www.historytoday.com
www.lifeloom.com
www.history.navy.mil
www.royalnavalmuseum.org
www.discoverynationalarchives.gov.uk
www.nam.ac.uk

www.records.nsw.gov.au/state-archives/research-topics/convicts

(John Barker – Ticket of leave holder No: 40/1634; Citation: 4/4222; Reel: 937 to page 95
John Smith – Conditional Pardon: Reel No: 4/4462; Reel 789; Page: 233-234 to page 95
Bartholomew Stephenson – Conditional Pardon, Item: (4/4453); Reel: 784; Page:121-122 to page 95
John Stewart/Steward – Conditional Pardon, Item: (4/4453); Reel: 784; Page: 123-124.)

Also available from Summerhill Books

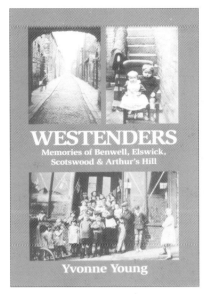

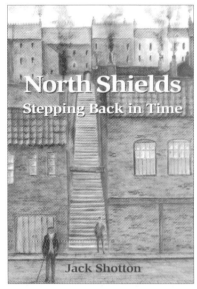

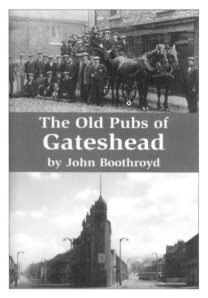

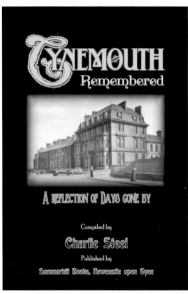

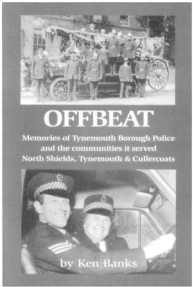

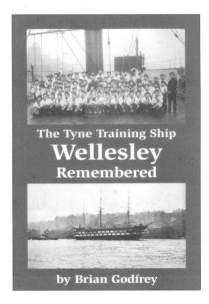

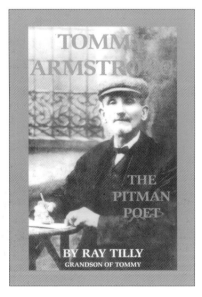

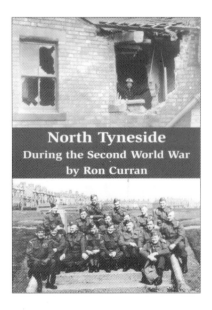

www.summerhillbooks.co.uk